UNLOCK CANADIAN WEALTH

The Friendly Roadmap to Finance and Investing in 2026.

Disclaimer:

The information provided in this book is for educational and informational purposes only. It is not intended as financial or investment advice and should not be construed as such. The author and publisher of this book are not financial advisors, and the content provided herein does not constitute professional financial advice. Readers are encouraged to consult with a qualified financial advisor or tax professional before making any financial decisions or investments based on the information presented in this book.

The author and publisher make no representations or warranties with respect to the accuracy, applicability, fitness, or completeness of the contents of this book. They disclaim any liability for any errors or omissions in the content or for any damages or losses arising from the use of the information provided herein. Readers use the information in this book at their own risk.

Contents

Chapter 1

Money Mindset and Budgeting

This opening chapter lays the groundwork for everything that follows, focusing on the psychological and practical foundations of personal finance. Before diving into savings plans and investments, it's essential to address your relationship with money—your mindset—and the core tool for managing it: budgeting. In Canada, where household debt-to-disposable income ratios edged up to around 174% in Q3 2025 amid ongoing pressures from inflation and housing, many are under financial stress from rising costs and obligations. A positive mindset, combined with effective budgeting, can help you break free from debt cycles, build wealth-accumulation habits, and achieve stability. We'll explore mindset shifts, budgeting techniques, tracking tools, and debt basics, with examples to make it applicable for beginners and those seeking refinement.

The Fundamentals of Money Mindset

Your money mindset is the set of beliefs and attitudes that shape how you handle finances—whether you see money as scarce and stressful or abundant and manageable. For beginners, common limiting beliefs like "I'll never get ahead" or "Rich people are lucky" can sabotage progress. A growth mindset, on the other hand, views challenges as opportunities to learn and improve.

Start by identifying your current mindset: Reflect on childhood influences (e.g., how your family discussed money) and track negative thoughts during financial decisions. Shifting to positivity involves gratitude, acknowledging what you have, and education, which reduces fear through knowledge.

A key concept: Financial habits compound like interest; small daily choices (e.g., skipping impulse buys) lead to significant results over time.

Behavioural tip: Watch for 'anchoring bias'—don't let that first big sale price fool you into thinking it's a deal if it breaks your budget.

Strategies to Cultivate a Positive Money Mindset

For those new to this, begin with simple practices:

Set clear, achievable goals: Use SMART criteria (Specific, Measurable, Achievable, Relevant, Time-bound), like "Save $5,000 for emergencies in 12 months."

Practice affirmations: Replace "I can't afford that" with "I'm choosing to prioritize my goals."

Track wins: Keep a journal of financial successes, no matter how small, to build momentum.

Use AI-powered apps: Tools like PocketGuard now use AI to predict spending patterns and nudge you away from impulse buys—think of it as a virtual accountability buddy.

Intermediates can delve deeper: surround yourself with positive influences, such as podcasts or books on financial psychology, and seek accountability through a friend or an online community.

Budgeting Basics: Taking Control of Your Cash Flow

Budgeting is the process of planning how to allocate your income to expenses, savings, and debt—ensuring you live within your means. A popular method for Canadians is the 50/30/20 rule: 50% on needs (rent, groceries), 30% on wants (dining out), and 20% on savings/debt.

If your 'wants' slice looks like it's on a diet, you're doing it right!

Steps to create a budget:

1. Calculate net income: After taxes and deductions.
2. List expenses: Fixed (mortgage) vs. variable (entertainment).
3. Categorize and adjust: Use apps to track in real-time.
4. Review monthly: Adapt as needed.

Consider this example: Alex, a young Toronto renter earning $60,000 annually, budgets $2,500 monthly for needs, $1,500 for wants, and $1,000 for savings/debt. This structure helps avoid overspending and builds a buffer.

Debt Basics: Understanding and Tackling It

Debt is borrowed money you repay with interest—common types in Canada include credit cards (~20-23%), student loans (0% on federal portions since 2023, provincial rates vary ~3-6%), and mortgages (~3-5% projected for 2026). With average household debt exceeding $200,000 (including mortgages), managing it is crucial.

Behavioural tip: Don't let this number scare you; it's like a marathon—start with small steps to chip away at it.

Two proven repayment strategies:

Debt Snowball: Pay off smallest debts first for quick wins and motivation, then roll payments to larger ones. Ideal for beginners needing encouragement.

Debt Avalanche: Target the highest-interest debts first to minimize total interest paid, then move down the list. It's best for long-term savings, though it may take longer to see progress.

Choose based on your mindset: Snowball for psychological boosts, avalanche for math-driven efficiency.

Potential Risks and How to Mitigate Them

Limiting beliefs can lead to avoidance or impulse spending—like hitting 'buy now' on that sale because it feels like a win. Poor budgeting risks debt accumulation if life throws curveballs (hello, unexpected car repair). Mitigate by automating savings transfers right after payday, building an emergency fund covering 3-6 months' expenses (start small, like Alex stashing $50/paycheque), and seeking free credit counselling from non-profits like Credit Canada if overwhelmed.

Behavioural tip: Combat loss aversion by celebrating 'no-spend' days—treat yourself to a walk in High Park instead of a latte run.

Self-Check: Mindset and Budgeting Basics

1. What's a growth mindset in finance?
2. Name the 50/30/20 rule categories.
3. Snowball vs. Avalanche: Which prioritizes interest savings?

If aligned, great; otherwise, review above.

Answers: 1. Viewing money challenges as learning opportunities, 2. Needs, wants, savings/debt, 3. Avalanche

Practical Tools and Next Steps

Budget Planner from the Financial Consumer Agency of Canada (FCAC): An interactive online tool to create a customized budget in simple steps, with charts and tips to see your cash flow clearly - itools-ioutils.fcac-acfc.gc.ca/BP-PB/budget-planner

Your Financial Toolkit from Canada Gov: Free online modules with budgeting lessons, worksheets, and calculators to build habits step-by-step - canada.ca/en/services/finance.html

Resources: CRA for tax tips [canada.ca/en/revenue-agency.html], FCAC (Financial Consumer Agency of Canada) for debt guides [canada.ca/en/financial-consumer-agency.html].

Action item: Assess your mindset with a quick journal entry, then use the FCAC Budget Planner to input one month's expenses. Bonus: Spot one sustainable swap, like biking to work, to save on transit. For extra help, chat with an AI like Grok (Grok.com) for simulated scenarios or mindset tips.

Next, we'll build on this with an overview of how to maximize savings in Canada.

Conclusion

In summary, a strong money mindset and solid budgeting practices form the bedrock of financial success, helping you navigate debt and develop effective habits. By adopting growth-oriented thinking, implementing structured budgets, and choosing the right debt strategy, you set yourself up for progress—whether starting fresh or advancing further. Use the tools and steps outlined to begin today, and remember, consistency is key to long-term mastery. Remember, slipping up? It's okay—finance is a marathon, not a sprint. Use these tools to get back on track.

Chapter 2

Maximizing Savings in Canada

This chapter provides an overview of Canada's primary savings options, building a foundation before we dive deeper into each plan in the following chapters. Planning for retirement—or other long-term goals like buying a home—can seem daunting, but Canada offers robust, tax-efficient vehicles to make it manageable. By understanding RRSPs, TFSAs, and FHSAs, you can optimize your savings, reduce taxes, and gain more control over your financial timeline. We'll outline the basics, benefits, and considerations, with practical examples to guide you. We'll keep it Canada-wide but sprinkle in Ontario scenarios, like how rising Toronto rents make these plans a lifesaver.

The Fundamentals

These plans are government-registered accounts designed to encourage saving by providing tax advantages. An RRSP focuses on retirement with upfront deductions, a TFSA offers tax-free flexibility for any purpose, and an FHSA targets first-time homebuyers with a hybrid approach. Together, they form a powerful trio for building wealth over time.

A key concept: Compound growth means your money earns returns on returns, accelerating over the years—but taxes can slow it down. These accounts minimize that drag, letting your savings work harder.

Eligibility and Contribution Limits

Eligibility is generally open to Canadian residents with earned income (for RRSPs) or aged 18+ (for TFSAs and FHSAs). Specifics vary: for FHSAs, you must be a first-time homebuyer (not owning a home in the last 4 years) and under 71.

Contribution limits are set annually and indexed to inflation. For 2026:

Plan	2026 Limit
RRSP	**Up to $33,810** or 18% of your 2025 earned income, whichever is less; unused room carries forward.
TFSA	**$7,000** annual; cumulative up to **$109,000** if eligible since 2009, and unused.
FHSA	**$8,000** annual, **$40,000** lifetime; up to **$8,000** unused room carries forward (must open an account to qualify).

Strategies to Maximize Savings

Beginners should prioritize consistent contributions—start small to build momentum. Intermediates can layer plans: Use RRSP for high-income years to maximize deductions, TFSA for flexible access, and FHSA for home goals.

Behavioural tip: Avoid 'lifestyle creep' by automating contributions—set it and forget it, so that raise doesn't vanish into extra takeout.

Consider this example: Alex, a 30-year-old Toronto renter earning $60,000, contributes $2,500 to his RRSP and $2,500 to his FHSA in 2026 (total $5,000 deduction). This drops his taxable income to $55,000, saving about $1,400 in taxes based on 2026 federal and provincial rates. He invests the refund in his TFSA via an S&P 500 ETF, potentially doubling it in 10 years at a 7% average return—all tax-free.

A bonus strategy: Transfer FHSA funds tax-free to your RRSP, even if maxed out, for extra deferral.

Withdrawals and Tax Considerations

RRSP: Withdrawals taxed as income; early pulls (before retirement) face withholding taxes and may bump your bracket.

TFSA: Tax-free anytime; room returns next year.

FHSA: Tax-free for home purchases within 15 years after opening the account; otherwise, transfer to RRSP or tax applies.

Plan withdrawals strategically to minimize taxes—e.g., in low-income years.

Potential Risks and How to Mitigate Them

Over-contributing triggers penalties (a 1% monthly penalty on excess contributions). Market dips can affect growth, so diversify. For FHSAs, missing the 15-year window means taxable closure unless transferred.

Mitigate by tracking via CRA tools and starting conservatively.

Self-Check: Key Plans

1. What's the 2026 RRSP max?
2. TFSA annual limit?
3. FHSA lifetime cap?

If aligned, great; otherwise, review above.
Answers: 1. $33,810, 2. $7,000, 3. $40,000

Practical Tools and Next Steps

Check limits: CRA My Account or call them at 1-800-959-8281.

Open accounts: At banks or brokerages like Wealthsimple or Questrade.

Action item: Calculate your room today and contribute $100 to test the waters.

Next, we'll explore TFSAs in detail, a complement to these for broader flexibility.

Conclusion

In summary, RRSPs, TFSAs, and FHSAs provide essential tax advantages for retirement and beyond, adaptable for beginners building basics or intermediates optimizing strategies. By focusing on limits, contributions, and smart withdrawals, you can enhance long-term security. Consult CRA resources or an advisor to personalize and take that first step toward mastery.

SECTION 1

Chapter 3

Tax-Free Savings Accounts (TFSA)

Building on the overview from the previous chapter, where we introduced Canada's key savings plans, let's take a closer look at the Tax-Free Savings Account (TFSA). Launched in 2009, the TFSA has become a cornerstone of personal finance for Canadians, offering a straightforward way to grow your savings without tax implications. It's particularly versatile, suitable for short-term goals like building an emergency fund or longer-term objectives such as supplementing retirement income. For beginners, it's an accessible entry point into investing; for those with more experience, it provides strategic advantages in tax planning. We'll cover the essentials here, including limits, strategies, and practical tips, with examples tailored to Ontario residents to make it relatable.

The Fundamentals of a TFSA

A TFSA allows you to contribute after-tax dollars, but all growth within the account—whether from interest, dividends, or capital gains—is entirely tax-free. Withdrawals are also tax-free and don't count as income, so they won't affect your eligibility for benefits like the Ontario Trillium Benefit or federal programs such as the GST/HST credit.

This makes it different from an RRSP, which offers upfront tax deductions but taxes withdrawals later (we'll compare the two in the next chapter). For starters, you can open a TFSA at most banks, credit unions, or online platforms like Wealthsimple or Questrade. It's not limited to cash savings; you can hold investments such as stocks, bonds, ETFs, or mutual funds in it, which we'll explore in Section 2.

A helpful way to think about it: In a standard savings account, taxes can erode your returns over time. In a TFSA, every dollar of growth stays with you, allowing compound interest to work more effectively.

Eligibility and Contribution Room

You're eligible for a TFSA if you're 18 or older, a Canadian resident, and have a Social Insurance Number (SIN). The contribution room begins accumulating from the year you turn 18 or become a resident, whichever is later.

The annual contribution limit for 2026 is $7,000. Unused room carries forward indefinitely, so if you've been eligible since 2009 and haven't contributed, your total room in 2026 could reach $109,000.

To help you estimate, here's a table showing the maximum contribution room in 2026 based on your birth year (assuming you turned 18 that year and have been a resident):

Birth Year	Year Turned 18	Max TFSA Room in 2026
1991 or earlier	2009	$109,000
1992	2010	$104,000
1993	2011	$99,000
1994	2012	$94,000
1995	2013	$88,500
1996	2014	$83,000
1997	2015	$77,500
1998	2016	$67,500
1999	2017	$62,000
2000	2018	$56,500
2001	2019	$50,500
2002	2020	$44,500
2003	2021	$38,500
2004	2022	$32,000
2005	2023	$25,500
2006	2024	$19,000
2007	2025	$12,000
2008	2026	$7,000

For an Ontario-specific context, if you're in a high-cost area like Toronto, maximizing your TFSA can help offset expenses like rent or property taxes while building wealth tax-free. Always confirm your exact room through the CRA's My Account portal to avoid penalties.

Strategies to Maximize Your TFSA

For those new to this, start with consistent contributions—perhaps by setting up automatic transfers from your paycheck to build the habit with minimal effort. As you gain confidence, consider investing rather than holding cash, especially with inflation projected at around 2% in 2026; low-risk options like GICs can provide steady, tax-free returns (more on fixed income in a later chapter).

If you have some investing experience, advanced tactics like covered calls—selling options on stocks you own to generate income—can enhance yields, all tax-free (details in the Derivatives chapter). The key is diversification to manage risk.

Consider this example: Alex, a 30-year-old Toronto resident earning $60,000, contributes his full $7,000 to his TFSA in 2026. He invests in a low-fee S&P 500 ETF for broad market exposure. Assuming a historical average return of 7% after fees, that could grow to around $14,000 in 10 years, all tax-free. Suppose in 2025, he withdrew $1,000 for unexpected costs; that contribution room was added back at the start of 2026, giving him flexibility without tax consequences.

One common pitfall: Over-contributing incurs a 1% monthly penalty on the excess, so double-check your room before adding funds.

Withdrawals and Tax Considerations

TFSAs offer unmatched flexibility—withdraw any time without penalties or tax withholding. The amount withdrawn is added back to your contribution room the following calendar year, not immediately, to prevent misuse. For strategic planning, consider withdrawing near year-end to reclaim room sooner.

Be mindful of foreign investments: Dividends from U.S. stocks, for instance, may be subject to a 15% withholding tax even in a TFSA, unlike in an RRSP, where treaties can reduce it. For beginners, focusing on Canadian assets initially simplifies things.

Potential Risks and How to Mitigate Them

While TFSAs are low-risk in structure, investments inside can fluctuate. If you sell at a loss, that contribution room is gone for good—no carry-forward like in taxable accounts. To counter this, reserve high-volatility investments for non-registered accounts, where losses can offset gains.

Additionally, frequent trading might attract CRA scrutiny if seen as business activity, potentially leading to taxation—aim for a long-term approach.

Self-Check: TFSA Basics

1. What's the 2026 annual limit?
2. When does the withdrawn room return?
3. Is growth taxable?

If these click, you're on solid ground; if not, revisit the sections above. Answers: 1. $7,000, 2. Next calendar year, 3. No

Practical Tools and Next Steps

To stay organized:

Use the CRA My Account online to track your room (updates by March for the prior year).

Call the CRA at 1-800-959-8281 for quick queries.

For setup, compare options at your bank or brokerage, such as Wealthsimple and Questrade.

Your action item: Log in to the CRA today and note your available room. Even a small contribution can start the momentum.

As we move to the RRSP chapter next, you'll see how it complements the TFSA for a balanced strategy. If budgeting or debt management feels like a prerequisite, we'll address those foundations in upcoming sections.

Conclusion

In summary, the TFSA stands out as a versatile, tax-efficient tool for Canadians, whether you're just starting or refining your portfolio. By leveraging its flexibility, contribution rules, and investment potential, you can build wealth more effectively—especially in Ontario's dynamic economy. Focus on staying within limits, diversifying wisely, and consulting resources like the CRA for guidance. With consistent use, it can play a key role in achieving your financial goals.

Chapter 4

Registered Retirement Savings Plan (RRSP)

Following our exploration of TFSAs in the previous chapter, let's turn to the Registered Retirement Savings Plan (RRSP), another pillar of Canadian retirement planning. Introduced in 1957, the RRSP is designed to encourage long-term savings by offering tax deductions on contributions and deferring taxes on growth until withdrawal. It's ideal for those in higher tax brackets during working years, as it reduces current taxes while allowing investments to compound tax-deferred. For beginners, it's a straightforward way to save for retirement; for intermediates, it provides opportunities for strategic tax management and spousal contributions. We'll cover the key elements, including limits, strategies, and tips, with practical examples to illustrate its use.

The Fundamentals of an RRSP

An RRSP is a registered account where contributions are tax-deductible, reducing your taxable income in the year you contribute. Growth inside the account—from interest, dividends, or capital gains—is not taxed until withdrawn, typically in retirement when you may be in a lower tax bracket.

This differs from a TFSA, which uses after-tax dollars but offers tax-free withdrawals (as discussed earlier). You can open an RRSP account at a bank, credit union, or an online brokerage like Wealthsimple or Questrade. It's not limited to cash; hold a diverse portfolio of investments, such as stocks, bonds, or ETFs, as we'll detail in Section 2.

A helpful way to think about it: Contributing to an RRSP is like getting a discount at the store from the government—the tax deduction lets you keep more money right away to invest, so your savings can grow bigger over time until you need them in retirement.

Eligibility and Contribution Room

You're eligible if you have earned income (e.g., salary, self-employment profits) and are under 71 (must convert to a RRIF by December 31 of the year you turn 71). The contribution room is calculated annually based on the prior year's income.

For 2026, the maximum limit is $33,810 or 18% of your 2025 earned income, whichever is less—to max out, you'd need about $187,833 in 2025 earned income. Unused room carries forward indefinitely. If you have a pension, a Pension Adjustment (PA) reduces your room—check your T4 slip.

To estimate, if your 2025 income was $100,000, your 2026 room is $18,000 (18%), assuming no PA. Always verify your RRSP contribution room in your Notice of Assessment (NOA) after filing taxes, or in CRA My Account anytime—it's best to check early in the year for planning. The deadline for RRSP contributions to count for the 2025 tax year is March 2, 2026.

Strategies to Maximize Your RRSP

Beginners: Contribute regularly via payroll deductions for automatic tax savings. As you progress, consider spousal RRSPs—contribute to your spouse's plan to split income in retirement and reduce overall taxes.

Advanced options: Use the Home Buyers' Plan (HBP) to withdraw up to $60,000 tax-free for a first home (repay over 15 years), or Lifelong Learning Plan (LLP) for up to $20,000 for education (repay over 10 years).

Consider this example: Alex, earning $60,000, contributes $5,000 to his RRSP in 2026. This deduction saves him about $1,250 in taxes (at a 25% marginal rate). He invests in a balanced ETF; at 7% annual growth, it could reach approximately $9,835 in 10 years (nearly doubling the original amount through compounding), tax-deferred. If married, a spousal contribution could optimize their joint taxes.

Another example for spousal RRSPs: Suppose Alex earns $80,000 while his spouse earns $40,000. Alex contributes $5,000 to his spouse's RRSP and claims the deduction on his higher-tax return. In retirement, withdrawals from the spouse's plan are taxed at a lower rate, splitting income and potentially saving the family $500+ in taxes annually—best when one partner has a significantly higher income or when pension disparities exist.

One common pitfall: Contributing without room—penalties apply, so confirm first.

Withdrawals and Tax Considerations

Withdrawals are taxed as income, with withholding taxes applied upfront (10-30% depending on the amount and province). Early withdrawals lose contribution room permanently and may affect benefits like Old Age Security (OAS), as RRSP withdrawals can trigger the OAS pension recovery tax (clawback) if your net income exceeds the threshold (e.g., $93,454 for July 2026-June 2027 payments).

At age 71, convert your RRSP to a retirement income option by December 31—it's like shifting your savings from growth mode to payout mode. The main choices are a Registered Retirement Income Fund (RRIF) for flexibility or annuitizing for steady income. Here's a quick breakdown to help you plan without penalties or extra taxes.

RRIF conversion: Your investments stay tax-deferred, but you must withdraw a minimum percentage annually starting the following year, based on the RRIF's January 1 value and your (or your spouse's) age. No tax withheld on the minimum, but it's taxable income. Withdraw more if needed, with possible withholding.

Annuitizing: Buy an annuity for guaranteed lifetime (or term) payments from an insurer—taxable but predictable, like a personal pension. Great for essentials, but you lose principal control.

Minimize taxes by withdrawing in lower-income years, such as during early retirement. For instance, Jordan from Windsor converts his $400,000 RRSP to a RRIF at 71, taking the $21,120 minimum in a low-income year to stay in a lower bracket—saving on taxes. Consult an advisor for your setup.

Be mindful: Employer group RRSPs may have vesting rules; check before withdrawing.

Behavioural tip: To avoid regret from early withdrawals, visualize your future self—use Canada gov retirement planner to simulate scenarios and stay disciplined [canada.ca/en/services/benefits/publicpensions/cpp/retirement-income-calculator.html].

Potential Risks and How to Mitigate Them

Like any savings tool, RRSPs have potential downsides—let's break them down simply so you can plan around them.

Higher taxes on withdrawal if retirement income rises: Remember, you get a tax break now, but withdrawals are taxed as income later. If your retirement pay (from pensions, CPP, or other sources) pushes you into a higher tax bracket, you could pay more tax than you saved upfront. Mitigation: Contribute when your income is high now and withdraw in lower-income years, such as during early retirement. For example, Jordan in Windsor plans to pull funds before his OAS starts, keeping his bracket low.

Market volatility affects growth: Your investments inside the RRSP can dip with stock market swings, potentially shrinking your nest egg short-term. Mitigation: To lower risk, shift toward stable options like Guaranteed

Investment Certificates (GICs), government bonds, or money market funds—these provide steady, predictable returns with less exposure to market ups and downs, like swapping a rollercoaster for a smooth train ride.

Over-reliance ignores TFSA flexibility: Putting everything in RRSPs means all growth is taxable on withdrawal, missing TFSA's tax-free perks for emergencies or non-retirement goals. Mitigation: Use both—RRSP for retirement, TFSA for flexibility. Think of it as not putting all eggs in one basket; blend them based on your timeline.

Self-Check: RRSP Basics

1. What's the 2026 max limit?
2. When must you convert to a RRIF?
3. Are withdrawals tax-free?

If aligned, great; otherwise, review above.
Answers: 1. $33,810, 2. Age 71, 3. No

Practical Tools and Next Steps

Track room: CRA My Account or 1-800-959-8281.

Calculators: Use CRA's online tools to estimate deductions.

For setup, compare at banks or brokerages like Wealthsimple and Questrade.

Your action item: Review your T4 for PA, calculate your room, and contribute if possible.

As we continue, the next chapter on FHSAs will show how it integrates with RRSPs for homebuying.

Conclusion

In summary, the RRSP is a tax-smart vehicle for retirement savings, offering deductions and deferral to boost long-term growth. By understanding eligibility, maximizing contributions, and planning withdrawals wisely, you can enhance your financial security—this is adaptable for beginners or intermediates. Leverage CRA resources and start small to build toward a prosperous future.

Chapter 5

First Home Savings Account (FHSA)

Building on the RRSP discussion in the previous chapter, let's examine the First Home Savings Account (FHSA), which is a newer tool introduced in 2023 to help first-time homebuyers. The FHSA combines RRSP-like tax deductions with TFSA-like tax-free growth and withdrawals, making it a hybrid option for saving toward a home down payment. It's particularly useful for younger Canadians facing high housing costs, as it offers a way to build savings efficiently. For beginners, it's an easy way to start tax-advantaged savings; for intermediates, it integrates well with other plans, such as RRSP transfers. We'll outline the essentials, including limits, strategies, and considerations, with examples to demonstrate its benefits.

The Fundamentals of an FHSA

An FHSA allows tax-deductible contributions (reducing your current taxable income) while providing tax-free growth on investments inside the account. Qualified first-home withdrawals are tax-free, blending the best of RRSPs and TFSAs.

This complements RRSPs (for broader retirement) and TFSAs (for flexibility), but is specifically for homeownership. Open an FHSA at banks, credit unions, or brokerages like Wealthsimple or Questrade. Invest in stocks, bonds, ETFs, or other qualified assets, as covered in Section 2.

A helpful way to think about it: The FHSA is like a targeted savings boost—deduct now, grow tax-free, and spend on your home without penalties.

Eligibility and Contribution Room

You're eligible if you're 18-71, a Canadian resident, and a first-time homebuyer (you **and** your spouse/common-law partner haven't owned a home in the current year or the prior four years). The account closes after 15 years, age 71, or a qualifying withdrawal—whichever comes first.

Contribution limits: $8,000 annual (unchanged for 2026), $40,000 lifetime. Unused room carries forward up to $8,000 per year (e.g., if you contribute $0 in 2025, you can do $16,000 in 2026), but you must open the account to start accruing room. Over-contributions are subject to a 1% monthly penalty.

To estimate, if you open in 2026 and max annually, you'll hit $40,000 in five years. Verify your contribution room via CRA My Account.

Strategies to Maximize Your FHSA

Beginners: Contribute steadily to claim deductions and build for a down payment. Intermediates: Transfer from RRSPs tax-free (up to limits) or use alongside the RRSP Home Buyers' Plan for up to $100,000 combined tax-free withdrawal.

A bonus strategy: Contribute to FHSA for deductions and growth, then transfer tax-free to RRSP (even if RRSP room is maxed) for extended deferral.

Consider this example: Alex, earning $60,000, contributes $8,000 to his FHSA in 2026. This saves him about $2,000 in taxes (at 25% marginal rate). Invested in a growth ETF at 7% annual return, it could grow to $11,200 in five years, tax-free, ready for a home purchase without penalties.

One common pitfall: Forgetting to open the account early—the contribution room only accrues once opened.

Withdrawals and Tax Considerations

Qualifying withdrawals (for a first home) are tax-free if used around the home acquisition closing date, and you meet eligibility. Non-qualifying withdrawals are taxed as income.

The funds in the FHSA account must be used within 15 years of inception; otherwise, transfer to an RRSP/RRIF tax-free or close the account with taxes on the growth.

Be mindful: Spousal FHSAs are individual—each partner can have their own for double limits.

Potential Risks and How to Mitigate Them

Housing market fluctuations could affect timing—save conservatively. Over-contributing penalties apply, and missing the 15-year window may result in potential taxes.

Mitigate by tracking via CRA, diversifying investments, and aligning with your home-buying timeline.

Self-Check: FHSA Basics

1. What's the annual limit?
2. Lifetime cap?
3. Are qualifying withdrawals taxed?

If aligned, great; otherwise, review above.
Answers: 1. $8,000, 2. $40,000, 3. No

Practical Tools and Next Steps

Track room: CRA My Account or 1-800-959-8281.

Calculators: Use bank tools for growth projections, or Canada Gov resources for free advice - canada.ca/en/financial-consumer-agency/services/buying-home.html.

For setup, compare at banks or brokerages like Wealthsimple and Questrade.

Your action item: Check eligibility on CRA's site and open if qualified—even without contributing to the start room.

As we proceed, the next chapter on RESPs will shift focus to education savings.

Conclusion

In summary, the FHSA is a targeted, tax-efficient account for first-time homebuyers, blending deductions and tax-free benefits to accelerate savings. By understanding eligibility, maximizing contributions, and planning withdrawals, you can leverage it effectively—whether you're starting your journey or integrating it with other plans. Use CRA resources for guidance and take steps today toward homeownership.

Chapter 6

Registered Education Savings Plan (RESP)

Shifting from home-focused savings in the previous FHSA chapter, let's explore the Registered Education Savings Plan (RESP), a dedicated tool for funding post-secondary education. Launched in 1974 and enhanced with grants in 1998, the RESP allows tax-deferred growth on contributions, with government incentives like the Canada Education Savings Grant (CESG) to boost savings. It's perfect for parents, grandparents, or guardians planning for a child's future studies, helping offset rising tuition costs (average undergraduate fees ~$7,000/year in 2025). For beginners, it's a simple way to save with bonuses; for intermediates, it offers family plan options and grant maximization. We'll detail the basics, limits, strategies, and tips, with examples to show its value.

The Fundamentals of an RESP

An RESP is a registered account where contributions (made by a subscriber) grow tax-deferred for a beneficiary's education. Earnings are taxed when withdrawn by the student (usually at a low rate), while grants add free government money.

This pairs well with other plans, such as TFSAs for flexible education funds or RRSPs for parental retirement. Open an RESP with a bank, credit union, or brokerage like Wealthsimple or Questrade. Invest in qualified assets like stocks, bonds, or ETFs, as discussed in Section 2. When you open an RESP, the provider typically applies for the CESG and other benefits, such as the CLB, on your behalf—verify this with them to ensure setup. Grants are deposited directly into the RESP account (not your personal account), so confirm with your provider that they're invested promptly rather than left in cash to maximize growth.

A helpful way to think about it: An RESP is like an education-specific savings accelerator—your contributions attract grants, and growth is sheltered until needed for school. Note that you don't need to be enrolled in a university or college program to qualify for grants; any eligible post-secondary program works, including trade schools, apprenticeships, or international programs. Check program eligibility on the Employment and Social Development Canada (ESDC) master list of designated educational institutions or the CRA website.

Eligibility and Contribution Room

Subscribers (anyone, no age limit) open for beneficiaries (typically under 21, Canadian residents with a SIN). No income requirement, but grants depend on family income.

Contribution limits: No annual cap, but a lifetime limit of $50,000 per beneficiary. Contributions must stop 31 years after the account is opened. Special needs plans (also called specified plans) are for beneficiaries who qualify for the Disability Tax Credit (DTC) due to severe and prolonged impairments; they allow contributions until the beneficiary is 59 and extend the plan duration up to 40 years (you can apply for an extension at the 31-year mark if eligible). Over-contributions incur a 1% monthly penalty on excess.

To qualify for a full $7,200 grants, contribute by December 31 of the year the beneficiary turns 17. Verify via CRA My Account or your RESP provider.

Strategies to Maximize Your RESP

Beginners: Contribute $2,500/year to max the CESG (20% match, $500/year, $7,200 lifetime per beneficiary). Low- and middle-income families get additional CESG (10-20% on the first $500) and the Canada Learning Bond (CLB: $500 initial + $100/year, up to $2,000, no contribution needed).

Intermediates: Use family plans for multiple kids (grants are applied per child, but funds are pooled together). Catch up on unused CESG grants (up to $1,000/year if room exists).

For example, suppose Priya has two children and opens a family RESP. She contributes $5,000 annually ($2,500 per child), attracting $1,000 total CESG ($500 each). If she missed contributions for one child in prior years, she can catch up by adding extra (up to $5,000/year total) to claim up to $1,000 CESG in one year, pooling the funds for whichever child needs them later.

One common pitfall: Missing grant deadlines—contribute early to maximize free money.

Withdrawals and Tax Considerations

Withdrawals fall into three types:

- Post-Secondary Education (PSE): Tax-free return of contributions to the subscriber.
- Educational Assistance Payments (EAP): Grants + growth, taxed to the student (usually low rate).
- Accumulated Income Payments (AIP): If unused for education, taxed to the subscriber + 20% penalty; can transfer to RRSP if room is available.

The beneficiary must be enrolled in a qualifying post-secondary program, either full or part-time. Withdrawals are possible up to 35 years after opening. Contributions must stop 31 years after the account is opened. It's recommended to withdraw government grants first to ensure they're used, then the profits (taxed at the student's rate), then the contributions (tax-free). There's a limit on EAPs in the first semester: $8,000 for full-time or $4,000 for part-time during the initial 13 consecutive weeks of enrollment; after that, unlimited amounts can be withdrawn as long as the student qualifies.

Potential Risks and How to Mitigate Them

If the beneficiary skips education, grants are lost, and AIP penalties apply—which can be mitigated by family plans (reallocate funds among siblings if one doesn't pursue studies) or AIP transfers (move accumulated income to your RRSP to avoid the 20% penalty, if you have RRSP room (up to $50,000). Market risks affect growth—diversify.

Over-contributing beyond $50,000 triggers penalties. Track progress annually via provider statements.

Self-Check: RESP Basics

1. What's the lifetime limit per beneficiary?
2. Max annual CESG?
3. Are EAPs taxed to the subscriber?

If aligned, great; otherwise, review above.
Answers: 1. $50,000, 2. $500, 3. No, to the student

Practical Tools and Next Steps

Apply for grants: Through your RESP provider, provide beneficiary SIN.

Track grant status: Review your RESP provider's annual statements or contact ESDC at 1-888-276-3624 for updates on deposits and eligibility - canada.ca/en/services/benefits/education/education-savings.html.

For setup, compare at banks or brokerages like Wealthsimple and Questrade.

Your action item: Gather your child's SIN, research providers online, and open an RESP today—even a $100 contribution can kickstart grants and growth.

Looking ahead to Section 2, we'll transition to investment types such as fixed income.

Conclusion

In summary, the RESP is a grant-boosted, tax-deferred plan for education savings, making it easier to fund future studies. By understanding eligibility, maximizing contributions and grants, and planning withdrawals, you can optimize benefits—suitable for beginners or families. Rely on CRA and providers for details, and start early to harness compounding for your loved ones' success.

Conclusion

SECTION 2

Chapter 7

Fixed-Income and Bonds Marketplace

As we conclude Section 1 on tax-advantaged accounts, Section 2 shifts to the building blocks of investing, starting with fixed-income securities and the bond marketplace. If you're new to investing, fixed-income simply means putting your money into loans where you get regular interest payments, like earning rent on your cash with lower risk than stocks (which can go up or down unpredictably). In 2026's economy, with the Bank of Canada holding its key interest rate at 2.25% and bond yields around 2.5-3.5% for safe options, these investments provide steady income during moderate growth. For beginners, they are a gentle way to start earning returns while protecting your principal; for intermediates, they add balance to a portfolio. We'll explain everything step by step, including how they work, types, strategies, and risks, with simple examples to build your knowledge from the ground up.

The Fundamentals of Fixed-Income Securities

Fixed-income securities are essentially loans you make to borrowers, such as governments or companies. In return, they pay you interest at set intervals and give back your original amount (principal) at maturity. Bonds are the classic example: You buy a bond with a "face value" (par value, usually $1,000 or $100), get "coupon" payments (interest, e.g., $30/year on a 3% bond), and receive the principal at "maturity" (the term's end, from 1 year to 30+ years).

Why choose them? They offer predictability—your payments are fixed, unlike stocks, where returns vary. Basic terms defined:

Coupon rate: Think of this as the bond's promised "paycheck"—it's the fixed (or sometimes variable) interest percentage the issuer agrees to pay you regularly, based on the bond's face value, usually $1,000, called "par". For example, a 5% coupon on a $1,000 bond means $50 in interest per year, split into payments, like semi-annually. It's set when the bond is issued and doesn't change with market prices, so it's your steady income stream, no matter what.

Yield (or Current Yield): This is your actual return on investment right now, factoring in what you paid for the bond. If you buy at a discount (below par, say $900 for a $1,000 bond), your yield is higher because you're getting the same coupons but for less money upfront—it's like snagging a sale item that still pays full dividends. Buy at a premium (above par, like $1,100), and the yield drops. Calculate it simply: annual coupon divided by current price.

Yield to Maturity (YTM): Imagine this as the complete road trip estimate for your bond if you hold it until the end (maturity date). It combines the coupon payments, any gain or loss from the price you paid versus par, and the time value of money—all annualized into one percentage. If rates fall, YTM might look appealing; if they rise, it could warn you off. It's great for long-term planning.

Duration: This measures the average time (in years) it takes to get your invested money back through coupons and principal, but it's also a sensitivity gauge: longer duration means the bond's price swings more with interest rate changes (like a long pendulum reacting dramatically to a push). For beginners, stick to shorter durations if you want stability—think of it as how "bouncy" your bond is in a changing economy.

Convexity: A step up from duration, this tells you how that sensitivity (duration) itself changes with significant interest rate shifts. Positive convexity (common in bonds) means prices rise more when rates fall than they drop when rates rise—it's like a safety net for forecasting wild price swings. For most starters, it's advanced, but it helps predict if your bond will curve in your favour if rates are volatile in 2026.

In Canada, these fit into RRSPs or TFSAs for tax perks (from Section 1). 2026 trends show GIC rates at 3-3.75% for 1-5 years, with bonds similar but tradeable for potential gains.

A useful way to think about it: You're the lender, earning interest for the risk, while the borrower uses your money for projects like building roads (government) or expanding business (corporate).

Eligibility and Accessibility

As long as you're a Canadian resident and at least the age of majority in your province, you're eligible—no special qualifications required. Think of it as a low-key entry: Just open a brokerage account to get started. Bonds aren't sold directly at bank branches like a savings account; instead, you buy them through brokerage services or get indirect exposure via mutual funds at your bank.

Minimums keep things accessible for beginners: Individual bonds typically require a minimum purchase of $5,000 (with face values starting at $1,000 and increments of $1,000 thereafter). If that feels steep, consider GICs (Guaranteed Investment Certificates, a reliable fixed-income cousin to bonds that lock in your money for a set term with guaranteed returns)—they often start as low as $500 (or even $100 at some providers) and can be bought directly from banks, credit unions, or brokerages. Think of it as a low-pressure way to test the waters.

Strategies to Maximize Fixed-Income Investments

Beginners: Go for GICs—choose non-redeemable for higher rates (locked in) or redeemable for early access (lower rates). Create a ladder investment by spreading investments across terms.

Intermediates: Ladder bonds for ongoing income; try inflation-linked or green bonds for eco-focused yields ~3.5%

Behavioural tip: To avoid over-reacting to rate changes, set a review schedule—quarterly checks prevent impulsive sells.

Consider this example: Alex invests $10,000 evenly across five GICs ($2,000 each) with maturities of 1 to 5 years at an average rate of 3.5%. Each year, one matures (e.g., the 1-year GIC pays back $2,000 principal + $70 interest), which he reinvests at the then-current rate. This strategy provides annual cash flow and reduces the risk of all money being stuck at a low rate if interest rates rise in 2026, given the stable environment.

A final example on buying a bond: Alex buys a $1,000 par Government of Canada bond with a 3% coupon for $980 (discount due to higher market rates). He earns $30 in annual interest; at maturity in 5 years, he receives $1,000 in principal, profiting $20 on price + interest—total YTM ~3.8%.

One common pitfall: overlooking callable bonds, which allow the issuer to repay early.

Liquidity and Tax Considerations

Liquidity: GICs can be difficult to cash out early due to penalties. Whereas bonds sell easily on the open market, prices may vary.

Tax: Interest taxed as income; you get a T-slip from your brokerage for easy filing. Capital gains if sold above cost. Foreign bonds may be subject to withholding taxes unless they are in an RRSP, where treaties often reduce or eliminate them—verify with your provider.

Potential Risks and How to Mitigate Them

Interest rate risk: Interest rates up, bond prices down—hold to maturity.

Credit risk: Issuer defaults; ratings from AAA (safest, low yields) to C (highest risk, higher coupon rates)—choose high-rated.

Inflation risk: Payments lose value—use inflation-protected bonds.

Call risk: Issuer repays early (often when rates fall, enabling refinancing at a lower rate), cutting your high-interest stream—check for call protection periods.

Diversify and use ratings from S&P or Moody's.

Self-Check: Fixed-Income Basics

1. What is a coupon rate?
2. If rates rise, bond prices?
3. GIC feature?

If aligned, great; otherwise, review above.

Answers: 1. Interest percentage, 2. Fall, 3. Guaranteed returns

Practical Tools and Next Steps

Rate comparison: Ratehub.ca or Bank of Canada site.

Calculators: Use brokerage Yield-to-Maturity tools.

For setup, compare at banks or brokerages like Wealthsimple and Questrade.

Your action item: Check a 1-year GIC rate and calculate interest on $1,000.

Next, equity with common vs. preferred shares.

Conclusion

In summary, fixed-income and bonds offer predictable income and safety, with 2026 stability making them a smart base. By understanding fundamentals such as types, pricing, and risks, you can invest confidently, whether you are a beginner or an intermediate investor. Use tools for research, start small for balance.

Chapter 8

Equity: Common vs Preferred Shares

Transitioning from the steady income of fixed-income investments in the previous chapter, let's explore equity—ownership stakes in companies through shares. If you're starting from scratch, equity investing means buying a small piece of a business, giving you a chance to share in its success (like profits or growth) but also exposing you to losses if the company struggles. In 2026, with the S&P/TSX Composite Index expected to rise by around 5% amid an economic recovery, shares can offer higher potential returns than bonds, but with greater volatility. The two main types are common and preferred shares, each suiting different goals. For beginners, this is your entry to company ownership; for intermediates, it adds growth to a portfolio. We'll cover the basics from the ground up, including what shares and dividends are, the differences between types, how they work, strategies, and risks, with clear examples to help it click.

The Fundamentals of Equity Shares

Equity shares are certificates of ownership in a publicly traded company—you become a shareholder, entitled to benefits based on the type. Companies first issue shares in the primary market (such as during an initial public offering, or IPO) to raise money directly for expansion, receiving funds from those initial buyers. After that, shares trade on the secondary market through stock exchanges like the Toronto Stock Exchange (TSX), where most investors access them via brokerages (such as online platforms from banks or apps like Wealthsimple or Questrade)—here, prices fluctuate constantly during trading hours based on supply, demand, company performance, or economic news, but the company doesn't get money from these ongoing trades.

Common shares: The most basic type, representing true ownership. You get voting rights, usually one vote per share at annual meetings to elect directors or approve significant changes, and may receive dividends; a portion of profits paid out, but not guaranteed—companies like Apple or RBC pay them quarterly if earnings allow; if profits drop, they can cut or skip them, as Tesla often does to reinvest in growth. Common shares also offer capital gains (sell for more than you paid) but bear the most risk if the company fails (last in line for assets).

Preferred shares: A hybrid between stocks and bonds, prioritizing steady income over ownership perks. You get fixed dividends (e.g., $1/share/year, paid before common) but usually no voting rights. If the company misses payments, cumulative preferred catches up later; non-cumulative does not. Preferred shares rank above common shares in bankruptcy—lower growth potential but more stable.

A helpful way to think about it: Common shares are like being a full partner in a business (voice and upside/downside); preferred shares are like a silent investor focused on reliable checks.

Getting Started and Buying Shares

No special requirements—anyone 18+ can open a brokerage account online, like Wealthsimple, Questrade, or bank-linked like TD Direct Investing. Banks themselves sell mutual funds, not individual stocks; for stocks, use a brokerage. The banks often have higher fees, $9.99/trade vs. $0 online.

Minimums are flexible: Buy one share (fractional even possible now), though "board lots" (100 shares) get better pricing; lots matter more for options trading (later chapter). Start with $100-500.

Buy via orders:

Market order: Buys/sells at the current market price—fast but no control if price shifts instantly.

Limit order: Sets your exact price (e.g., buy only if $50 or less)—gives control but may not execute if the market doesn't hit it.

Strategies to Maximize Equity Investments

Beginners: Invest in blue-chip common shares—stable giants like Canadian banks (RBC, TD) or the global "Magnificent 7" (Apple, Amazon, Microsoft, etc.) — for reliable dividends, growth, or both. Hold long-term to weather dips: This means keeping shares for years (5-10+), riding out short-term price drops (dips) from market fluctuations, as quality companies tend to recover and grow over time—avoiding panic sales locks in losses.

Intermediates: Blend preferred shares for income stability with common shares for appreciation.

A key strategy is Dividend Reinvestment Plans (DRIPs): Instead of cash dividends, they automatically buy more shares (e.g., a $50 dividend on a $50 stock buys one extra share, compounding your holdings over time without additional money from you—great for growth through reinvestment).

Consider this example: Alex, a beginner, buys 20 common shares of RBC at $100 each ($2,000 total investment). Over a year, the price rises to $110, giving him a $200 capital gain if he sells (20 shares x $10 increase). Plus, RBC pays a quarterly dividend of about $1 per share, so he receives $80 annually (20 shares x $4/year). He enrolls in DRIP, using those dividends to automatically buy fractional shares, growing his position without additional cash.

One common pitfall: Buying trendy stocks without research—focus on fundamentals like the company earnings.

Dividends

Dividends are portions of a company's profits distributed to shareholders, typically paid quarterly (e.g., $0.50 per share means $50 for 100 shares). Not all companies pay them—mature, profitable ones, like banks, do to reward investors, while growth companies like Tesla often skip them to reinvest in expansion. If a company cuts or suspends dividends (e.g., during tough times), your income drops, and the stock price might drop too as investors sell.

For preferred shares, dividends are usually fixed (set rate like 5% of par value) and prioritized (paid before common), making them more reliable—cumulative types, accumulate missed payments for later payout, which is appealing for income-focused investors.

Stock Split

A stock split increases the number of shares while lowering the price per share, keeping your total value the same—it's like cutting a pie into more slices. Companies do this when prices get too high (e.g., over $500) to make shares more affordable, attract small investors, and boost liquidity (easier trading). For example, Tesla did a 3-for-1 split in 2022: If you owned one share at $900, it became three at $300 each (still $900 value)—this made it accessible to more buyers, increasing trading volume.

A reverse stock split does the opposite: Combines shares to raise the price (e.g., 1-for-10 turns 10 shares at $1 into one at $10). Companies use this to meet exchange listing requirements (e.g., minimum $1 price on NYSE), appear more stable to investors, or reduce volatility from penny-stock trading. However, it can signal financial trouble if done to avoid delisting.

Tax Considerations

In Canada, dividends from eligible corporations (large public Canadian companies) receive favorable tax treatment: They're "grossed up" by 38% for calculation (e.g., $100 dividend treated as $138 income), but you get a dividend tax credit to offset taxes, lowering your effective rate (e.g., in a 20% bracket, pay ~12% on the grossed-up amount). Non-eligible dividends (from small private firms) are taxed as regular income without the credit. Foreign dividends are taxed at a higher rate (15% withholding, unless held in an RRSP in most cases, where treaties often waive it for the US and similar). Capital gains (profits from selling shares) are 50% taxable (e.g., $200 gain = $100 taxed). Hold in registered accounts, like RRSPs, to defer taxes.

Example 1 (Canadian eligible): Alex receives a $100 dividend from RBC (eligible). Grossed up to $138, taxed at 25% bracket ($34.50), but credit reduces to ~$20 net tax—net $80 (effective ~20%).

Example 2 (Canadian non-eligible): Alex receives $100 from a small Canadian firm (non-eligible, no credit). Taxed as regular income at 25% ($25). Net: $75 (effective 25%).

Example 3 (Foreign US): $100 from Apple. After 15% U.S. withholding ($85 left), taxed as non-eligible at 25% (~$21.25), total effective tax

~36%—net $63.75. If in RRSP, no withholding, net $100 immediate, taxed on withdrawal.

Final Comparison of the Three Options

Scenario	Gross Dividend	Withholding Tax	Canadian Tax (at 25% Bracket)	Net After-Tax	Key Notes
Canadian Eligible	$100	$0	~$20 (after credit)	$80	Most efficient due to tax credit; ideal for large Canadian firms.
Canadian Non-Eligible	$100	$0	$25	$75	No credit; taxed like regular income—common for small firms.
Foreign US (Non-Registered)	$100	$15	~$21.25	$63.75	Withholding hurts; hold in RRSP to avoid it (net $100 immediate).

Overall, Canadian-eligible dividends save the most (~20% effective tax rate vs. 25-36% for others); RRSPs optimize foreign dividends by waiving withholding taxes.

Potential Risks and How to Mitigate Them

Market risk: Share prices drop with bad news or recessions—mitigate by diversifying across sectors (e.g., tech, energy, finance, healthcare; don't put all in tech if AI hype fades).

Dividend risk: Cuts if profits fall (e.g., during downturns)—check the company payout ratio (dividends as % of earnings; under 60% is sustainable, meaning the company retains enough for growth—find this information on Yahoo Finance or company reports).

Liquidity risk: Low-traded shares are hard to sell quickly. Check average daily volume on stock quotes; high liquidity = millions traded/day, like RBC; low = thousands for small firms.

Inflation risk: Dividends/gains may not outpace rising costs (e.g., 3% dividend < 4% inflation = real loss)—pair them with growth-oriented shares (companies expanding fast, like tech, to increase value over time).

Long-term holding and regular reviews reduce overall risks.

Self-Check: Equity Basics

1. What common shares include?
2. What is the preferred shares' advantage?
3. What is a DRIP benefit?

If aligned, great; otherwise, review above.

Answers: 1. Voting rights, 2. Priority dividends, 3. Auto-reinvestment of dividends

Practical Tools and Next Steps

Research: Yahoo Finance or Questrade tools for quotes/dividends.

Screener: Use free online tools like Yahoo Finance stock screener for blue-chip stocks.

For setup, compare brokerages like Wealthsimple and Questrade.

Your action item: Look up RBC's price and dividend yield on $1,000—it's a reliable Canadian dividend stock with over 150 years of payments.

Next, equity transactions, such as cash/margin accounts.

Conclusion

In summary, common and preferred shares offer ownership and income potential, with 2026 markets favouring blue chips for stability. By understanding types, dividends, splits, and risks, you can invest smartly—beginner or intermediate. Use tools for research, start with one share to learn.

Chapter 9

Equity Transactions

Building on the overview of common and preferred shares in the previous chapter, let's examine equity transactions—the processes for buying, selling, and managing shares on the market. For beginners, this is like learning the rules of the game: How to enter positions, place orders, and handle risks without getting burned. In 2026, with online brokerages offering free or low-cost trades and apps allowing instant execution, it's easier than ever, but mistakes can be costly. For intermediates, it's about using tools like margin to amplify strategies. We'll cover account types, positions and orders, with detailed examples to illustrate.

The Fundamentals of Equity Transactions

Equity transactions are the actions you take to trade shares, from simple buys to complex strategies. You execute them through a brokerage on exchanges like the TSX, where prices are determined by supply and demand. Key terms:

Bid price: The highest price buyers are willing to pay right now.

Ask price: The lowest price sellers are willing to accept.

Spread: The gap between bid and ask (e.g., bid $99.90, ask $100.10 = $0.20 spread)—narrow spreads indicate high liquidity and lower costs.

Account types define what you can do:

Cash accounts: Basic and safe; trade only with your deposited funds—no borrowing.

Margin accounts: Advanced; let you borrow from the brokerage to trade more, but require approval (e.g., experience quiz), usually minimum ~$2,000 equity, and ongoing "maintenance" (keep 30-50% of your total position value as your own equity, or face margin calls to add funds or sell).

Positions are your bets:

Long position: Buy shares expecting the price to rise (available in cash or margin; okay in TFSA if not excessive trading).

Short position: Sell borrowed shares expecting the price to fall (only in margin; not in registered accounts like RRSP/TFSA due to CRA rules).

A helpful way to think about it: Cash accounts are like paying with your wallet; margin is credit card trading—long is "buy and hold hope," short is "sell first, buy later."

Getting Started and Account Types

Open a brokerage account—online, like Wealthsimple/Questrade for low fees, or through your bank like TD Direct (higher costs). No special eligibility for cash accounts; however, margin usually needs additional verification.

Cash accounts: No minimum beyond deposits; safe for beginners.

Margin accounts: Usually require a minimum initial equity of $2,000 to open (varies by broker); you can borrow up to 50% of the purchase price for eligible stocks (e.g., with $10,000 cash, buy $20,000 in shares by borrowing $10,000 at around 7% interest).

For maintenance, keep at least 30% equity in the total position value to avoid a margin call (your broker demanding more cash or sales to restore the ratio). Equity here means your own money in the position after subtracting the loan.

For example, starting with $20,000 shares ($10,000 yours + $10,000 borrowed), equity is 50%. If shares drop to $15,000, equity becomes $5,000 ($15,000 value - $10,000 loan), or 33%—still above 30%, so okay. But if they drop to $14,000, equity is $4,000 ($14,000 - $10,000), or about 29%—below 30%, triggering a margin call that requires you to add funds or sell to cover it.

Strategies to Maximize Equity Transactions

Beginners: Use cash with market orders (buy/sell at the current price); add a stop-loss (auto-sell if the price hits the low limit) or a good 'til cancelled (order stays until filled or cancelled).

Intermediates: Use margin for long positions in dips; add a stop-buy for shorts (auto-buy if price hits high to limit losses).

Behavioural tip: To curb over-trading, limit checks to weekly—apps' notifications can fuel impulsivity, so turn them off for calm decisions.

Long example: Alex in cash takes a long position in 10 RBC shares at $100 ($1,000 total). He expects growth from earnings; price rises to $110 over months, so he sells for $1,100, profiting $100 (capital gain).

Short example (illustration only, not recommended): Alex in a margin account borrows 10 declining stock shares at $100, sells them for $1,000. Price falls to $80; he buys back for $800, returns them, profiting $200 minus fees/interest. If the price rose to $120, he'd buy back for $1,200, losing $200+—and potentially unlimited losses if the rise continues.

One common pitfall: Ignoring spreads—wide spreads eat profits on low-liquidity stocks.

Tax Considerations

Taxes on equity transactions in Canada are straightforward but important to understand, as they can significantly impact your net returns. Let's break it down step by step for clarity.

First, **capital gains and losses**: When you sell a share for more than you paid (a capital gain), only 50% of the profit is taxable. For example, if you buy a share for $100 and sell it for $300, your $200 profit is a capital gain, and you'll pay tax on just $100 of it at your marginal tax rate (the rate on your last dollar of income, which varies by bracket and province—e.g., at 25%, you'd owe $25). Conversely, if you sell at a loss (buy at $300, sell at $100 = $200 loss), you can use that loss to offset gains in the same year, or carry it back three years or forward indefinitely to reduce future taxes on capital gain. This encourages long-term investing by taxing only half of the gain while allowing losses to offset gains.

Second, **dividends**: These are taxed as income, but Canadian dividends from eligible corporations (most large public companies) get favourable treatment through the dividend tax credit. The dividend is "grossed up" by 38% for calculation (e.g., a $100 dividend is treated as $138 income), taxed at your marginal rate, but the credit reduces the effective tax (e.g., in a 25% bracket, net tax might be ~$20, leaving $80). Non-eligible dividends (from small private firms) are taxed like regular income without the credit. Foreign dividends are often subject to a 15% withholding tax at source, plus Canadian tax.

Finally, **registered accounts** (like RRSPs or TFSAs) defer or eliminate immediate taxes: Gains, losses, and dividends grow tax-free inside until withdrawn (deferred in RRSPs, tax-free in TFSAs). This makes them ideal for holding equities in the long term.

Overall, plan transactions with taxes in mind—use registered accounts for deferral, offset losses against gains, and favour eligible Canadian dividends for the credit to keep more of your returns.

Potential Risks and How to Mitigate Them

Execution risk: Orders don't fill (e.g., limit order is too strict)—use market order for speed.

Leverage risk: Margin calls or automatic liquidation if value drops below maintenance requirement (e.g., 30%)—keep buffer cash to avoid this. In fast markets, brokers may liquidate positions without calling first, selling your assets to repay the loan and cover debts.

Short risk: Unlimited losses if price rises—set stop-buy orders.

Fee risk: High trades eat profits—choose low-fee brokers.

Mitigate by practicing with demo accounts first and setting price alerts.

Self-Check: Equity Transactions Basics

1. What is a cash account limit?
2. What is a long position bet?
3. What is a margin call?

If aligned, great; otherwise, review above.

Answers: 1. Your deposited funds, 2. Price rise, 3. Broker forces action when equity is too low due to losses

Practical Tools and Next Steps

Order practice: Broker demo accounts.

Track: Yahoo Finance for quotes.

For setup, compare brokerages like Wealthsimple and Questrade.

Your action item: Open a demo account and place a market order for a blue-chip stock.

Next, derivatives like options.

Conclusion

In summary, equity transactions enable buying/selling shares, with 2026 tech making it seamless. By grasping accounts, positions, orders, and risks, you can trade confidently—beginner or intermediate. Use tools for practice, start small to gain experience.

Chapter 10

Derivatives

This chapter introduces derivatives—financial tools that can add leverage and flexibility to your investing, but they're not for everyone. If you're new to this, think of derivatives as contracts based on something else, like betting on the direction of a stock price without owning the stock itself. In Canada's 2026 market, with steady economic growth projected at around 2% and volatility from global events, derivatives like options and futures can help hedge risks or speculate, but they come with higher stakes. We'll break it down simply, with examples using our Ontario friends, analogies to make it relatable, and tips to avoid common pitfalls. Remember, these are advanced—start small if you're curious, and always consult a professional.

The Fundamentals of Derivatives

Derivatives are agreements between two parties in which the value "derives" from an underlying asset, such as stocks, interest rates, commodities (e.g., oil or wheat), or even cryptocurrencies. It's like a side bet on a hockey game—you're not playing, but you're wagering on the outcome. Common types include options (giving the right, but not the obligation, to buy/sell) and futures (obligating both sides to trade at a set price at a later date).

A key concept: Leverage means you control a large position with less money upfront, amplifying gains (or losses). For beginners, this can feel exciting but risky—like using a magnifying glass to focus sunlight; it intensifies everything.

Here's a quick table comparing main types:

Type	Description	Example Underlying Assets
Options	Contracts giving the buyer the right (but not the obligation) to buy or sell an asset at a set price by a certain date, in exchange for a premium paid to the seller. The seller, however, is obligated to fulfill the trade if the buyer exercises the option.	Stocks, indices, currencies
Futures	Obligation to buy/sell at a set price on a future date; no premium, but margins required.	Commodities (oil, gold), bonds

Terminology

Before diving deeper, let's define some key terms to make this more straightforward:

Strike Price (or Exercise Price): The fixed price at which the underlying asset can be bought or sold if the option is exercised.

Premium: The fee paid by the option buyer to the seller for the rights in the contract—non-refundable, like an insurance premium.

Expiration Date: The deadline for exercising the option; after this, the contract ends.

Exercise: Acting on the option to buy (call) or sell (put) the asset at the strike price.

In-the-Money: When exercising would be profitable (e.g., for a call, asset price > strike; for a put, asset price < strike).

Out-of-the-Money: When exercising wouldn't be profitable (opposite of in-the-money).

At-the-Money: When the asset price equals the strike price—no immediate profit.

Intrinsic Value: The built-in profit if exercised now (e.g., for a call: asset price - strike, if positive).

Time Value: The extra premium value due to uncertainty and time left until expiration (premium = intrinsic value + time value).

Offset Transaction: Closing a position by taking the opposite trade to cancel it out.

Options come in two main styles: American (exercisable at any time before expiration) and European (exercisable only on the expiration date). Most stock options in Canada are American-style.

Exploring call and put options offers investors four strategic choices:

Speculating on Price Increase

Call Option - Long Call (option buyer): The buyer acquires the right (but not the obligation) to purchase an underlying asset at a predetermined price and time, paying a premium to the seller.

Put Option - Short Put (option seller - writer): Sellers sell a put option, obligating themselves to buy the underlying asset at a predetermined price and time if the buyer chooses to exercise, receiving a premium from the buyer.

Speculating on Price Decrease

Call Option - Short Call (option seller - writer): Sellers sell a call option, obligating themselves to sell the underlying asset at a predetermined price and time if the buyer chooses to exercise, receiving a premium from the buyer.

Put Option - Long Put (option buyer): The buyer acquires the right (but not the obligation) to sell an underlying asset at a predetermined price and time, paying a premium to the seller.

Getting Started and Account Types

To trade derivatives in Canada, start by opening a brokerage account if you don't have one—most major banks and online platforms offer them. Eligibility is open to residents aged 18+, but you'll need specific approval for options or futures, where brokers (regulated by CIRO) review your experience and finances to ensure readiness.

Account types and key steps:

Cash Accounts: Limited to buying options only; no margin for selling or futures.

Margin Accounts: Required for advanced strategies like selling options or futures; allows borrowing but increases risk.

Approval Process: Submit a questionnaire; levels range from basic (e.g., covered calls) to advanced (e.g., naked options).

In 2026, with TSX volatility around 15-20%**,** expect stricter margins (3-10% for futures, varying for options) during uncertain times.

Strategies to Use Derivatives

Beginners: Stick to basic hedging—use options to protect existing investments, like insurance on your portfolio. Intermediates: Speculate on trends or generate income via premiums.

Behavioural tip: Avoid greed-driven trades; set rules like "only risk 1% of my portfolio" to curb impulsivity—journaling helps build discipline.

Here are some relatable examples:

Call Option Strategy (Covered Call): Alex, our young Toronto renter who owns 1,000 shares of XYZ Company bought at $50 each, expects the price to stay steady or dip slightly in 2026. He sells a call option with a $55 strike price for a $2 per-share premium, pocketing $2,000 upfront. If XYZ stays below $55 by expiration, the option expires worthless, and Alex keeps the premium as extra income—like renting out his shares for a fee. He can repeat this for ongoing cash flow. If the price rises above $55 and the buyer exercises, Alex sells at $55, making a profit of ($55 - $50) x 1,000 = $5,000, plus the $2,000 premium, for a total of $7,000. This works great in a TFSA for tax-free gains, and if XYZ pays dividends, Alex keeps those too.

Put Option Strategy (Cash-Secured Put): Priya, the Ottawa family planner, uses some leisure money in her TFSA to potentially buy 100 shares of XYZ Company (current price $55) but only if it drops to $50—her target for a value play. She sells a put option with a $50 strike for a $2 premium per share, earning $200 immediately. She sets aside $5,000 (cash-secured) in her account to cover the potential purchase. If XYZ stays above $50, the option expires worthless, and Priya keeps the $200 as income—boosting her leisure funds without buying. If it falls below $50 and is exercised, she buys at $50, but her net cost is $48 per share after the premium, like getting a discount on shares she wanted anyway. This is a smart way to generate income while waiting for a dip, and it fits well in a TFSA for tax-free premiums.

Futures Contract Example: Imagine a Saskatchewan farmer (we'll call him Sam) growing wheat and worried about falling prices due to a good harvest in 2026. He enters a futures contract to sell his wheat at $8 per bushel in six months. No premium upfront, but he posts an initial margin of $5,000 (say 10% of contract value) with a $4,000 maintenance margin. His counterparty (a buyer like a food processor) does the same. Accounts settle daily: If wheat prices drop $0.50 per bushel on a given day (a gain for Sam as seller), his account increases, and the buyer's decreases. If Sam's balance drops below $4,000, he adds funds. At expiration, they transact at $8—locking in Sam's revenue regardless of market drops, like pre-booking a sale to avoid price surprises.

Withdrawals and Tax Considerations

Derivatives don't have "withdrawals" like accounts, but profits/losses settle at expiration or close. Taxes: Gains from options/futures are capital gains (50% taxable) if held as investments, or business income if frequent trading. In registered accounts (TFSA/RRSP), it's tax-free/deferred. Track via T5008 slips, a tax form your broker sends reporting your securities transactions, like sales and purchases, to help with your tax return. Use CRA tools for estimates.

Potential Risks and How to Mitigate Them

Derivatives can lead to significant losses—leverage works both ways, and time decay erodes option value. Market volatility in 2026 could amplify this.

Mitigate by starting with paper trading (simulations), diversifying, and using stop-loss orders. If overwhelmed, consult a qualified financial advisor. AI trend: Use AI tools like Grok for scenario simulations to test strategies risk-free.

Self-Check: Derivatives Basics

1. What's leverage in derivatives?
2. Name two option types.
3. Futures vs. Options: Which requires obligation from both parties?

If aligned, awesome; otherwise, revisit above.

Answers: 1. Controlling large positions with less money, amplifying gains/losses, 2. Call and put, 3. Futures

Practical Tools and Next Steps

Research: Use investopedia.com for free guides on options/futures.

Simulators: Reliable options like Questrade's practice account, or Investopedia's stock simulator—test strategies risk-free.

Action item: Assess your risk tolerance with a free quiz from sites like GetSmarterAboutMoney.ca/tools/, then sign up for a practice account with a trusted broker, such as Questrade, to try out derivatives trading risk-free.

Next, we'll dive into mutual funds for diversified, hands-off investing.

Conclusion

In summary, derivatives like options and futures offer powerful ways to hedge, speculate, or boost income, but they're best for those comfortable with risk. By understanding basics, using smart strategies, and mitigating pitfalls, you can incorporate them thoughtfully—whether generating income like Alex or hedging like Sam. Start slow, stay informed, and remember: knowledge reduces fear, turning complexity into opportunity.

Chapter 11

Mutual Funds

Shifting gears in Section 2, this chapter explores mutual funds—a popular way for beginners to dip their toes into investing without picking individual stocks or bonds. Think of them as a group road trip: Everyone chips in, a professional driver (fund manager) handles the route, and you share the journey's ups and downs. In Canada's 2026 landscape, with mutual fund assets projected to exceed $2 trillion amid steady economic growth, these funds offer diversification and ease, but fees and choices matter. We'll cover the basics, how to get started, strategies with our Ontario examples, and more to help you decide if they're right for your portfolio.

The Fundamentals of Mutual Funds

Mutual funds pool money from many investors to buy a diversified mix of assets like stocks, bonds, or both, managed by professionals. It's like a shared investment pot where the manager aims to grow it based on the fund's goals—whether income, growth, or balance. For beginners, this means less stress than solo stock-picking; the pros handle research and trades.

A key concept: Diversification spreads risk across many holdings, like not putting all your eggs in one basket. If one stock dips, others might rise, smoothing returns. In 2026, amid lingering market volatility from global shifts, funds holding 60-100 securities across industries offer built-in safety.

Here's a table of common types:

Type	Description	Risk Level	Example Focus
Money Market	Short-term, safe investments like treasury bills for steady, low returns.	Low	Liquidity and preservation.
Fixed-Income	Bonds and similar for regular income; less volatile than stocks.	Low-Medium	Government or corporate bonds.
Balanced	A mix of stocks and bonds for moderate growth and income.	Medium	All-weather stability.
Equity	Stocks for higher growth potential; more ups and downs.	Medium-High	Canadian or global companies.
Specialty	Targeted themes like tech or regions are exciting but niche.	High	ESG or sector-specific.

Getting Started and Account Types

To trade mutual funds in Canada, start by opening a brokerage account if you don't have one—most major banks and online platforms offer them.

Eligibility is open to residents aged 18+, with no strict approvals needed like for derivatives, but you'll want to align with your risk tolerance.

Account types and key steps:

Non-Registered: Basic cash accounts for general investing; taxable on gains.

Registered: Hold funds in TFSA, RRSP, or FHSA for tax perks—ideal for long-term goals.

Robo-Advisor or Advisor-Led: Automated platforms for hands-off setup, or human advice for personalized picks.

In 2026, expect average management expense ratios (MERs) around 1.5-2% for active funds, down from prior years due to competition from low-cost options. Shop around via fund prospectuses for transparency.

MER stands for Management Expense Ratio. Think of it as the "cost of running the show" for a mutual fund (or even an ETF). It's an annual fee, expressed as a percentage of the fund's total assets, that covers things like the fund manager's salary, administrative costs, marketing, and other operational expenses. Basically, it's what you pay the pros to pick and manage the investments inside the fund, so you don't have to.

Strategies to Maximize Your Mutual Funds

Beginners: Focus on low-cost index funds that track markets like the TSX—simple and effective. Intermediates: Build a mix based on goals, rebalancing yearly.

Behavioural tip: Resist chasing hot funds; past performance isn't a guarantee—stick to your plan to avoid emotional buying and selling.

Consider this example: Alex, our young Toronto renter, starts with $5,000 in a balanced mutual fund via his TFSA and adds $100 monthly. At a 1.8% MER and 6% average return, it could grow to ~$12,800 in five years after fees.

Another: Priya, the Ottawa family planner, uses an equity fund in her kids' RESP for their education. She contributes $200 monthly, attracting grants (like the CESG at 20% on contributions up to $2,500/year per child), and the diversified holdings (e.g., Canadian banks and tech) aim for 7-8% growth. Over 15 years, this could grow to around $80,000-$88,000, helping cover rising tuition costs.

For Jordan, the Windsor retiree. He invests $100,000 in a fixed-income fund in his RRSP for steady 4% yields, setting up monthly distributions to generate about $333 per month (or $4,000 annually) in retirement income. This provides reliable payouts without stock volatility—perfect for his low-risk phase, like a steady pension supplement to cover everyday expenses.

Withdrawals and Tax Considerations

Redeeming units—think of it as cashing out your share of the pool—is straightforward: You sell them back to the fund at the net asset value (NAV), which is the total worth of the fund's investments divided by the number of units, calculated at the end of each trading day. It's like a daily "closing price" update to keep things fair. In non-registered accounts, taxes hit two ways, but not twice on the same income: Capital gains (50% of profit taxable) only on sales, while distributions (dividends, interest, or fund gains from its internal transactions) pass through to you and are taxed that year—even if reinvested or unsold, like an automatic paycheck tax. (Reinvested distributions increase your adjusted cost base to avoid double-counting later.) That's why it's recommended to hold mutual funds in registered accounts like TFSAs (entirely tax-free) or RRSPs (deferred until withdrawal) to skip annual taxes on those fund activities. Retirees like Jordan can use systematic withdrawals (e.g., 4% yearly in chunks) for steady cash without big tax surprises.

Potential Risks and How to Mitigate Them

Funds can lose value in market downturns, and high MERs (over 2%) erode returns over time. Fund manager underperformance can be another pitfall.

Mitigate: Choose low-fee passive funds, diversify across types, and review annually. AI trend: Platforms like Wealthsimple use AI for personalized fund picks and rebalancing, making it easier for beginners.

Self-Check: Mutual Funds Basics

1. What's diversification in mutual funds?
2. Name two fund types.
3. Active vs. Passive: Which typically has lower fees?

If aligned, great; otherwise, review above.

Answers: 1. Spreading investments to reduce risk, 2. E.g., equity and fixed-income, 3. Passive

Practical Tools and Next Steps

Fund Research: Use morningstar.com/funds for ratings and comparisons or fundresearch.fidelity.com for detailed fund info.

Track: Yahoo Finance or Google Finance for real-time fund quotes and performance charts.

For setup, compare providers like RBC Mutual Funds, TD Asset Management, or robo-advisors such as Wealthsimple Invest.

Action item: Choose a mutual fund type that aligns with your goals (e.g., equity for growth), then use Morningstar.ca to research one fund's details like MER and holdings, and calculate a sample $1,000 investment's potential growth over 5 years at 6% return using the GetSmarterAboutMoney calculator - getsmarteraboutmoney.ca/calculators/mutual-fund-fee-calculator/.

Next, we'll explore exposure to cryptocurrency using ETFs for a modern twist.

Conclusion

In summary, mutual funds provide an accessible entry into diversified investing, blending ease with professional management to help achieve goals like retirement or education. By grasping types, fees, and smart strategies—like Alex's balanced approach or Priya's growth focus—you can build steadily. Remember, start small, watch costs, and stay consistent; over time, this teamwork turns savings into growth.

Chapter 12

Exposure to Cryptocurrency Using ETFs

Wrapping up Section 2, this chapter dives into cryptocurrency exposure through ETFs—a smarter, more regulated way to tap into digital assets without the hassle of direct ownership. If you're curious about crypto but wary of wallets and hacks, think of these ETFs as a guided tour: They let you ride the waves of Bitcoin or Ethereum while pros handle the details. In Canada's 2026 market, with crypto adoption projected to grow amid stabilizing regulations and potential new ETF approvals for altcoins like Solana and Cardano, these ETFs offer volatility with built-in safeguards. Remember, crypto's exciting but risky—approach with eyes open and only what you can afford to lose.

Cryptocurrency

Cryptocurrency—often called "crypto"—is a form of digital money that runs on blockchain technology, which is basically a super-secure, tamper-proof, shared digital ledger spread across thousands of computers worldwide. No central bank or government controls it, allowing direct peer-to-peer trades without intermediaries. Popular ones like Bitcoin (the original "digital gold"), Ethereum (which powers smart contracts, like automated agreements), or Cardano (a research-driven, proof-of-stake platform emphasizing scalability, sustainability, and real-world applications such as supply chain tracking and solving financial inclusion issues) can skyrocket in value but also crash hard due to market hype, regulations, or tech shifts—think of it as a high-stakes rollercoaster for diversification. In this chapter, we're zeroing in on a beginner-friendly way to get involved: through ETFs, which package crypto like a basket of stocks, letting you invest via your regular brokerage without the headaches of wallets, keys, or direct buying. It's a smart, regulated entry point for Canadians curious about this evolving asset class.

The Fundamentals of Exposure to Cryptocurrency Using ETFs

Crypto ETFs are exchange-traded funds that track the price of cryptocurrencies like Bitcoin or Ethereum, holding the assets directly or via futures. It's like buying a ticket to a concert (the crypto market) without dealing with the crowd—your investment moves with the crypto's value, but in a familiar stock-like format on the TSX. For beginners, this means easier access than buying crypto outright, with regulatory oversight from bodies like the OSC or SEC.

A key concept: Volatility is crypto's hallmark—prices can swing 10-30% in a day due to news or sentiment, but ETFs add diversification if multi-asset. In 2026, top funds like BlackRock's iShares Bitcoin Trust or Fidelity's Advantage Bitcoin ETF hold billions in assets, reflecting growing mainstream appeal. Note that most crypto ETFs are denominated in USD, so consider currency exchange impacts when trading from Canada.

Here's a quick table of popular crypto ETFs:

Type	Description	Risk Level	Example ETFs (2026 Projections)
Spot Bitcoin	Directly holds Bitcoin for real-time tracking; no futures.	High	BlackRock iShares Bitcoin ETF (IBIT), Fidelity Advantage Bitcoin ETF (FBTC)
Spot Ethereum	Tracks Ether; newer but gaining traction.	High	Fidelity Advantage Ether ETF (FETH), BlackRock iShares Ethereum Trust (ETHA)
Multi-Crypto	Mixes BTC, ETH, XRP, SOL, and ADA for broader exposure.	High	Grayscale CoinDesk Crypto 5 ETF (GDLC)

Getting Started and Account Types

To get exposure to crypto via ETFs in Canada, start by opening a self-directed brokerage account—platforms like Questrade or Wealthsimple are a good place to start, as banks typically don't offer direct access to these. Eligibility is open to residents aged 18+, with no special approvals needed beyond standard investing requirements, but ensure your broker allows trading in these ETFs (often US-listed).

Account types and key steps:

Non-Registered: Basic for taxable trading; good for short-term plays.

Registered: Can be used in a TFSA or RRSP for tax advantages —ideal since crypto gains can be sheltered, but note these are high-risk; **losses permanently reduce contribution room without recovery.**

In 2026, expect MERs of 0.4-1% for top funds, competitive given inflows exceeding $10 billion in assets—review fund fact sheets for holdings.

Strategies to Maximize Your Crypto ETF Exposure

Beginners: Allocate a small portion (5-10%) of your portfolio to a spot Bitcoin ETF for simple exposure. Intermediates: Pair with stable assets or use for hedging.

Behavioural tip: Crypto's hype can trigger FOMO (Fear Of Missing Out, that nagging feeling you'll regret not jumping in during a surge)—set buy/sell rules upfront and avoid checking prices obsessively to stay rational.

Consider this example: Alex, our young Toronto renter, dips in $1,000 into the BlackRock iShares Bitcoin ETF (IBIT) via his TFSA. If Bitcoin rises 50% in 2026 (as some forecasts suggest amid adoption), his investment grows to $1,500 tax-free—like catching a wave without getting wet.

Another example: Priya, the Ottawa family planner, adds Grayscale CoinDesk Crypto 5 ETF (GDLC) to her kids' RESP for long-term growth, contributing $100 monthly. It diversifies her kids' fund with a mix of top cryptos, aiming for 20-30% annual returns in bull markets but ready for dips.

Jordan, the Windsor retiree, buys the Fidelity Advantage Bitcoin ETF (FBTC) in his non-registered account for modest speculation, limiting it to 2% of his portfolio to preserve stability.

Withdrawals and Tax Considerations

Selling ETF shares is like any stock—done via your broker at market price, with liquidity during trading hours.

Taxes: Treated as capital gains (50% taxable) in non-registered accounts; full income if business-like trading. In TFSA/RRSPs, gains are tax-deferred or tax-free, making them well-suited to crypto volatility. Track with T5008 slips (broker reports transactions); CRA views crypto ETFs as commodities, so no special rules beyond standard investing.

Potential Risks and How to Mitigate Them

Crypto ETFs inherit crypto's wild swings—Bitcoin could drop 30% on regulatory news—and added fees (0.5-1%) plus potential tracking errors. Emerging risks in 2026 include tighter rules on stablecoins or global tax transparency.

Mitigate: Diversify, invest long-term, and use dollar-cost averaging. Start small and educate via free resources. AI trend: Tools like Grok can simulate crypto scenarios.

Self-Check: Crypto ETF Basics

1. What's a spot crypto ETF?
2. Name two risks of crypto ETFs.
3. Tax perk in TFSA?

If aligned, great; otherwise, review above.

Answers: 1. Directly holds the crypto for price tracking, 2. Volatility, regulatory changes, 3. Tax-free growth

Practical Tools and Next Steps

Research: BlackRock.ca for iShares ETFs, Fidelity.ca for Advantage series, or Grayscale.com for GDLC details.

Track: Use CoinMarketCap ETF tracker coinmarketcap.com/etf/ for real-time prices or ETF.com etf.com/topics/cryptocurrency for charts.

For setup, compare brokers like TD Direct Investing, RBC Direct Investing, or Questrade that offer access to these ETFs.

Next, we'll kick off Section 3 with interest rates and their economic impact.

Conclusion

In summary, crypto ETFs offer a gateway to digital assets with less complexity, blending excitement with structure for diversified portfolios. By understanding fundamentals, using strategies like Alex's cautious entry or Priya's long-term play, and managing risks, you can explore this space thoughtfully. Start informed, invest wisely, and remember: Crypto's potential is huge, but patience turns volatility into opportunity.

SECTION 3

Chapter 13

Interest Rate and Its Impact on the Economy

Kicking off Section 3, this chapter explores interest rates—the unsung heroes (or villains) of the economy that influence everything from your mortgage payments to stock market trends. If you're new to this, picture interest rates as the economy's thermostat: The Bank of Canada (BoC) adjusts them to keep things from overheating or freezing up. In Canada's 2026 market, with the key policy rate projected to likely remain at or near 2.25% early in 2026 amid moderate growth and lingering inflation pressures, understanding their impact can help you make smarter decisions on saving, borrowing, and investing. We'll break it down with simple explanations, Ontario examples, and practical tips to help you build your confidence.

The Fundamentals of Interest Rates

Interest rates are the cost of borrowing money or the reward for saving it, set as a percentage. In Canada, the Bank of Canada (BoC) controls the key policy rate, which influences everything else—like prime rates at banks (around 4.45% in 2026 projections) or mortgage rates. For beginners, think of it as the price tag on money: Low rates make borrowing cheap (boosting spending), high rates make borrowing expensive (encouraging saving).

A key concept: The overnight rate is the BoC's primary tool, targeting 2% inflation. Overnight borrowing refers to short-term loans banks make to each other to meet daily reserve requirements—it's like banks lending spare cash overnight at the BoC's set rate. This ripples to consumers: If the overnight rate rises, banks pass on higher costs through increased prime rates, making variable-rate loans (e.g., lines of credit or adjustable-rate mortgages) more expensive for you, potentially adding hundreds to your monthly payments and curbing spending.

When inflation rises (e.g., due to supply chain issues), rates go up to cool demand; when growth slows, rates drop to stimulate it. Inflation is calculated using the Consumer Price Index (CPI), which tracks price changes in a fixed "basket" of about 700 goods and services representing average Canadian household spending (e.g., food, housing, transportation). StatCan surveys prices monthly across cities, weights them by spending patterns (e.g., housing is 30% of the basket), and computes the year-over-year increase to get the inflation rate. The CPI uses 2002 as its benchmark year (set to 100), meaning a "basket" of goods and services that cost 100 in 2002 would cost about 165.30 in October 2025, reflecting cumulative inflation.

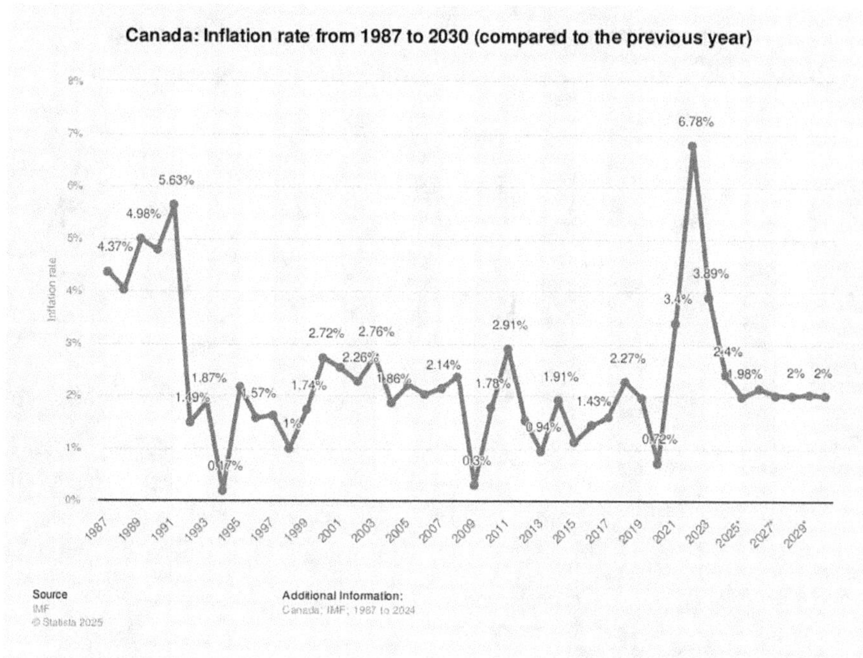

Why not keep rates low all the time? While low rates spur growth, they can fuel runaway inflation (eroding purchasing power), create asset bubbles (like overheated housing), and discourage saving (why save if returns are tiny?). The BoC aims for balance to sustain long-term stability.

In 2026, with no further cuts expected and possible hikes if the economy heats up, this balance targets steady GDP growth around 2%. GDP (Gross Domestic Product) growth measures how much the economy expands annually—the total value of goods and services produced in Canada. Positive growth (e.g., 2%) signals more jobs and prosperity; stagnation or decline signals a slowdown.

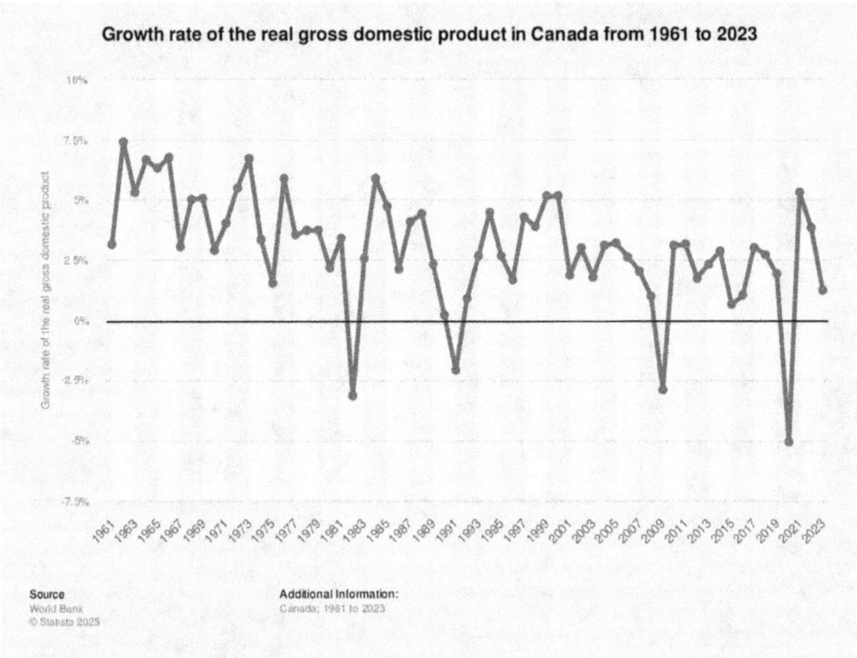

Here's a quick table of rate types:

Rate Type	Description	2026 Projection	Example Impact
Policy Rate	BoC's benchmark for banks' lending overnight.	2.25%	Sets tone for all rates.
Prime Rate	The benchmark interest rate banks use for their most creditworthy customers, serving as a base for various loans.	4.45%	Affects variable mortgages.
Mortgage Rate	For home loans, fixed or variable.	3-4.5%	Low rates make buying easier.
Savings Rate	Interest on deposits like GICs.	1-3%	Higher rates boost savings growth.

Recent data

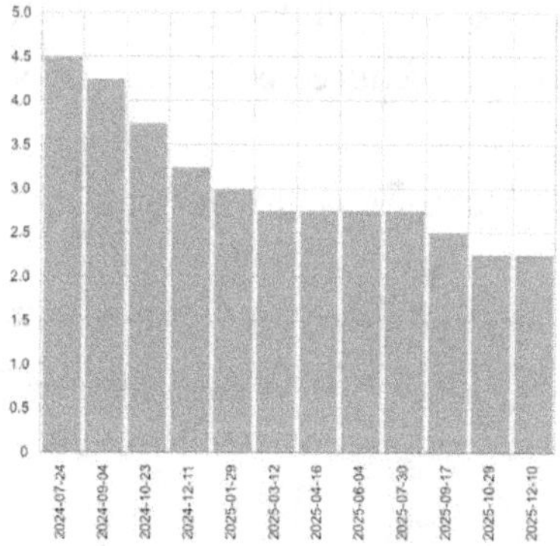

Date*	Target (%)	Change (%)
December 10, 2025	2.25	---
October 29, 2025	2.25	-0.25
September 17, 2025	2.50	-0.25
July 30, 2025	2.75	---
June 4, 2025	2.75	---
April 16, 2025	2.75	---
March 12, 2025	2.75	-0.25
January 29, 2025	3.00	-0.25
December 11, 2024	3.25	-0.50
October 23, 2024	3.75	-0.50
September 4, 2024	4.25	-0.25
July 24, 2024	4.50	-0.25

Bank of Canada interest rate

How Interest Rates Affect the Economy

The BoC meets eight times a year to set rates, responding to data such as inflation (target: 2%) and unemployment (around 6.5% in 2026 projections). High rates curb spending (e.g., fewer car loans), slowing growth but taming inflation. Low rates encourage borrowing (e.g., business expansions), spurring jobs but risking bubbles.

Note: The prime rate directly impacts variable-rate products (e.g., adjustable mortgages or lines of credit), whose payments fluctuate with changes in the prime rate. Fixed rates are more influenced by bond market yields—long-term government bonds reflect investor expectations of future rates and inflation, so if bonds rise, fixed mortgage rates follow suit independently of prime.

In Ontario, where housing costs are high, a steady 2.25% rate could stabilize Toronto's market after 2025's rebound by keeping borrowing affordable without fueling wild price jumps, helping first-time buyers enter without overextending. But hikes might squeeze Canadian manufacturers, if exports slow—higher rates increase borrowing costs for equipment or operations (e.g., a $500,000 loan jumping from 4% to 5% adds $5,000 yearly interest), raising product prices and reducing competitiveness against U.S. rivals with lower rates, potentially leading to reduced orders and layoffs.

Strategies for Investors in Different Rate Environments

Beginners: In stable rates like 2026's, focus on balanced portfolios—mix bonds (which benefit from higher yields) and stocks (which grow with the economy). Intermediates: Adjust based on trends; lock in GICs if rates peak.

Behavioural tip: Avoid panic from rate news—FOMO on "hot" investments during lows can lead to losses; review your plan quarterly for calm decisions.

Consider this example: Alex, our Toronto renter earning $60,000, sees steady rates and parks his $10,000 emergency fund in a 3% 1-year GIC, earning $300 interest safely. This beats low-yield savings accounts (1-2%), and he monitors his credit card (at a fixed high rate around 20%, which typically doesn't fluctuate with BoC hikes as issuers set them independently) to pay off balances quickly and avoid compounding interest.

Priya, in Ottawa, uses low borrowing costs to refinance her variable mortgage at 4%, dropping her monthly payment by $200 to $300 on a $400,000 loan. Combined with budget tweaks (e.g., cutting dining out by $200), this frees up around $500 total for her TFSA contributions, where she adds to a balanced ETF aiming for 6% average growth to build her family's buffer amid stable rates—potentially turning $6,000 yearly into $7,200 after one year.

Jordan, the Windsor retiree with $200,000 in savings, shifts 40% ($80,000) to 5-year bonds yielding 3.5%, locking in $2,800 annual income tax-efficiently in his RRSP. This protects against potential hikes that could dent stock returns (e.g., if rates rise, bond prices fall but his fixed yield stays), while keeping 60% in equities for growth in a moderate economy, providing a steady $10,000 yearly drawdown without depleting principal.

Potential Risks and How to Mitigate Them

Rate changes can hurt: When it rises, it increases loan costs (e.g., variable mortgages up 0.5%), and when it falls, it erodes savings yields. In 2026, unexpected interest rate hikes driven by strong growth could hit borrowers.

Mitigate: Diversify (don't put all-in on bonds), use fixed-rate loans, and build buffers—like an emergency fund of 3-6 months' expenses in a high-interest savings account to cover surprises without selling investments at a loss. AI trend: Use BoC's online tools or ask Grok for simulations of rate changes on your budget to plan proactively.

Self-Check: Interest Rates Basics

1. What's the BoC's inflation target?
2. High interest rates help control what?
3. At low rates, what gets cheaper?

If aligned, awesome; otherwise, revisit above.
Answers: 1. 2%, 2. Inflation, 3. Borrowing

Practical Tools and Next Steps

Track Rates: Bank of Canada website for announcements or RateHub.ca for comparisons.

Calculators: Use FCAC's mortgage tool to simulate impacts itools-ioutils.fcac-acfc.gc.ca/MC-CH/MortgageCalculator.aspx.

Action item: Check your current loan/savings rates, then use a BoC calculator to see how a 0.5% change affects your budget—plan one adjustment this month, canada.ca/en/services/finance/tools.html.

Next, we'll explore the business cycle and how economies ebb and flow.

Conclusion

In summary, interest rates shape the economic landscape, influencing your daily finances from loans to investments. By understanding their role—like the BoC's steady hand in 2026—you can strategize effectively, whether saving like Alex or refinancing like Priya. Stay informed, adapt thoughtfully, and remember: Rates fluctuate, but smart habits keep you ahead.

Chapter 14

The Business Cycle: How the Economy Moves in Cycles

Building on our look at interest rates, this chapter dives into the business cycle—the natural ups and downs of the economy that affect jobs, prices, and your investments. If you're new to this, imagine the economy as a rollercoaster: It climbs during good times, peaks at the top, dips into tougher periods, bottoms out, and then recovers before climbing again. In Canada's 2026 outlook, we're likely in an expansion phase following the 2025 recovery, with steady GDP growth around 2% amid moderate inflation and stable rates. But projections suggest a potential slowdown risk in mid-2026 from global factors. Understanding these cycles helps you time your decisions better, such as when to invest aggressively or play it safe. We'll explain it simply, with Ontario examples using our friends, analogies, and graphs to make it relatable.

The Fundamentals of the Business Cycle

The business cycle is the economy's recurring pattern of growth and slowdown, typically lasting 5-10 years, driven by factors like consumer spending, business investment, and government policies. It has five main stages:

Expansion: The "good times" where GDP grows, jobs increase, and spending rises—think booming Toronto tech sectors hiring more.

Peak: The top, where growth slows as inflation heats up and resources stretch thin.

Contraction (Recession): A downturn characterized by falling GDP, rising unemployment, and reduced spending—often triggered by high interest rates or shocks such as pandemics.

Trough: The bottom, where things stabilize at low levels.

Recovery: The rebound, where activity picks up, leading into the next expansion—jobs return, confidence builds, and growth resumes.

It's like seasons: Spring (expansion) brings growth, summer (peak) is hot but unsustainable, fall (contraction) cools off, winter (trough) is tough, and early spring (recovery) signals renewal. In Canada, cycles are tracked by StatsCan using GDP data; recessions are defined as two consecutive quarters of negative growth.

A key concept: Cycles aren't predictable but follow patterns—expansions average 4-5 years, recessions 1-2. In 2026, expect continued expansion if rates stay low, but watch for a mid-year peak if inflation rises above 2%.

To visualize, here's a standard graph of the business cycle with the five stages labelled:

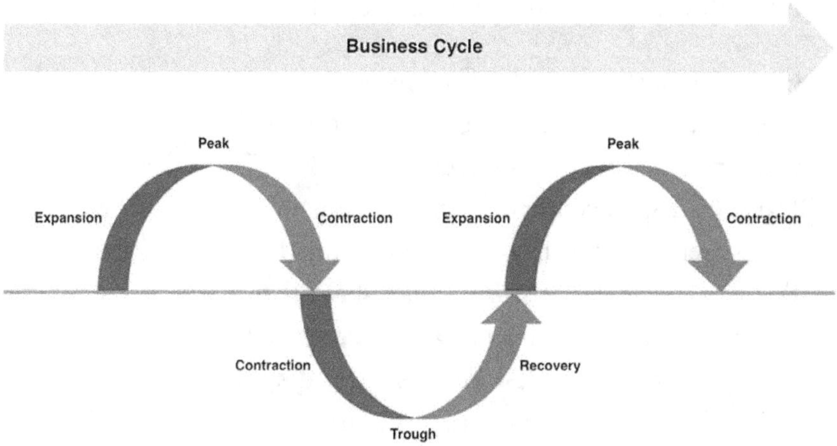

Business Cycle - Definition, How to Measure and 5 Different Stages

How the Business Cycle Affects the Economy and Investments

Cycles ripple through everything: In expansions, low unemployment (e.g., around 6.5% in 2026 projections) boosts wages and stock markets, but inflation rises. Recessions hit hard—jobs lost, stocks drop 20-30%, but bonds shine as safe havens. In Ontario, expansions fuel Toronto's housing market, but 2026 projections show stability amid affordability pressures, with potential declines of 3-5%, while contractions squeeze industries and trigger slowdowns.

The 2008-2009 Global Financial Crisis: Triggered by the U.S. housing collapse, Canada entered a contraction, with GDP dropping to around 3% in late 2008-early 2009 and unemployment spiking to above 8%. Exports fell, hitting manufacturing, but strong banks led to a quick recovery by 2010.

The 2020 COVID-19 Recession: Lockdowns caused a record 11.5% GDP plunge in Q2 2020, unemployment hitting around 13%. Government aid spurred recovery, with GDP rebounding 11.9% in Q3 2020, leading to expansion by 2021.

Analyzing S&P/TSX During Recessions

To show why you don't need to fear business cycles if you diversify and hold long-term, let's analyze the S&P/TSX Composite Index—Canada's main stock market benchmark—during recessions. This index tracks about 250 large Canadian companies across sectors such as finance, energy, and materials, representing roughly 70% of the Toronto Stock Exchange's market capitalization. Historical data show that while recessions cause short-term drops, the index has always recovered and grown over time, rewarding patient investors. For instance, despite multiple downturns since 1957 (when the index began), the S&P/TSX has delivered an average annual return of about 10% (including dividends), turning $1,000 invested in 1970 to around $200,000 by 2025—far outpacing inflation.

Analyzing S&P/TSX During Recessions: Recessions are tough, with the index often falling 20-50% as economic slowdowns hit corporate earnings and investor confidence. But recoveries follow, often within 1-3 years, driven by stimulus, lower rates, and rebounding demand. Here's a look at three major ones:

1. **2000-2002 Dot-Com Recession:** Triggered by the tech bubble burst, Canada's economy contracted with GDP dropping ~1.5% in 2001. The S&P/TSX fell ~43% from its 2000 peak (~11,400) to a trough of ~6,500 in October 2002, as tech and telecom stocks tanked. Yet, it recovered fully by 2004, climbing back above 11,400 by 2006—holders who stayed in saw ~100% gains in the next expansion phase.
2. **2008-2009 Global Financial Crisis:** Sparked by the U.S. housing crash, Canada entered a recession, with GDP shrinking by ~3.3% in Q4 2008-Q2 2009. The S&P/TSX plunged ~50% from its June 2008 high (~15,000) to ~7,500 in March 2009, hammered by falling commodity prices and banking fears. Recovery was swift: It regained

pre-crisis levels by 2011 and, by 2025, had tripled to ~31,000—long-term investors captured massive growth post-rebound.

3. **2020 COVID-19 Recession:** Lockdowns caused a sharp ~5.2% GDP drop in Q1-Q2 2020. The S&P/TSX crashed ~37% from February highs (~17,900) to ~11,200 in March amid uncertainty. Thanks to government aid, it rebounded quickly, surpassing pre-COVID levels by November 2020 and hitting new records above 22,000 by 2022—demonstrating how even severe shocks fade over time.

The lesson? If you diversify (e.g., mix TSX stocks with bonds or global funds) and hold through cycles, short-term losses (average recession drawdown ~30%) turn into long-term wins. Since 1957, the index has risen from ~500 to over 31,000 by late 2025, a ~62x increase, despite 11 recessions. Patience beats trying to time the market.

Strategies for Each Phase

Diversify across phases—don't chase highs. Intermediates: Adjust allocations based on indicators such as rising unemployment, which signals contraction.

Behavioural tip: Cycles trigger greed in peaks (buying overpriced stocks) or fear in troughs (selling low)—journal your emotions to stick to a long-term plan and avoid knee-jerk moves.

In expansion (2026 likely): Grow with stocks; Alex adds to his TFSA equity ETF as jobs boom.

At peak: Shift to bonds or GICs; Priya locks in GICs before rates fall.

In contraction: Buy undervalued assets; Jordan holds cash for bargains.

At trough: Invest aggressively; all prepare for recovery.

In recovery: Build momentum; focus on growth stocks as the economy rebounds.

AI tip: Use Grok to model cycle impact on your portfolios.

Potential Risks and How to Mitigate Them

Cycles can surprise: recessions wipe out 10-20% of portfolios, expansions breed bubbles. In 2026, a sudden slowdown from global trade issues could hit exports.

Mitigate by rebalancing annually, maintaining 6 months' emergency cash, and using dollar-cost averaging. AI trend: Ask Grok to analyze cycle indicators or simulate portfolio performance in phases.

Self-Check: Business Cycle Basics

1. Name the five stages.
2. What thrives in expansions?
3. How to mitigate risks?

If aligned, awesome; otherwise, revisit above.

Answers: 1. Expansion, peak, contraction, trough, recovery, 2. Stocks and jobs, 3. Diversify and rebalance

Practical Tools and Next Steps

Track the Cycle Basics: Head to Statistics Canada's main page for economic data and search for "GDP" or "unemployment rate" to see monthly updates. It's like checking the weather; look at the numbers to spot if things are growing (expansion) or slowing (contraction).

Calculators: Use the Bank of Canada's free tools to play with numbers, like how inflation affects your savings—just enter basic info and see the results - bankofcanada.ca/rates/related/inflation-calculator/.

Action Item: Visit Trading Economics website, look at the "GDP Growth Rate" chart, see if the economy is expanding or contracting, and think about one easy tweak, like boosting your emergency savings by $50 this month if things look like they're peaking. No significant changes needed—just get a feel for it!

Conclusion

In summary, the business cycle's rhythms guide the economy and your finances—expansions build wealth, contractions test resilience. By spotting stages with tools like graphs and adapting strategies, like Alex growing in good times or Priya preparing for peaks, you stay ahead. Cycles repeat, but knowledge turns them into opportunities—keep learning and stay steady.

Chapter 15

Investment Analysis

By now, you've got the basics down—savings accounts, bonds, stocks, and even a peek at crypto ETFs. But how do you decide if a particular investment is worth your hard-earned cash? That's where investment analysis comes in. Think of it like test-driving a car before buying: You check under the hood (fundamentals) and watch how it handles on the road (technical trends). This chapter is your beginner's toolkit for evaluating investments, whether you're eyeing TSX stocks for your TFSA or mutual funds for retirement. We'll keep it straightforward, with real-world examples from Ontario folks like Alex (our Toronto renter building his first portfolio) and Priya (the Ottawa mom planning for her kids' education)—no jargon overload—just practical steps to build confidence. Let's turn those "what ifs" into wise choices.

The Fundamentals of Investment Analysis

Investment analysis is the process of evaluating an asset—such as a stock, bond, or fund—to determine whether it aligns with your goals and risk tolerance. It's not about predicting the future perfectly (no one has a crystal ball), but using data to make informed guesses. There are two main approaches: **fundamental analysis**, which examines a company's health and the broader economic picture, and **technical analysis**, which studies price patterns and market behaviour. Combining them gives you a fuller view, like using both GPS and road signs on a drive from Toronto to Ottawa.

Before diving in, let's touch on some market theories that explain why analysis matters—or sometimes doesn't. These ideas help set expectations:

Efficient Market Hypothesis (EMH): This says markets are "efficient," meaning stock prices already reflect all available information. So, beating the market consistently is tough—most folks do better with index funds. But in practice, not everyone's info is perfect, so analysis can spot edges.

Random Walk Theory: Prices move randomly, like a drunkard's stagger. Past performance doesn't predict the future, so don't chase "hot" stocks based on history alone.

Rational Expectations Hypothesis: Assumes investors are logical and learn from mistakes. In reality, emotions often sneak in—more on that later.

These theories remind us: Markets are mostly fair, but human quirks create opportunities. For 2026, with AI speeding up info flow, EMH feels even truer, but sustainable factors (like climate impact) are adding new layers.

Behavioural tip: Watch for "confirmation bias"—seeking info that backs your hunch, like ignoring bad news on a stock you like. Counter it by listing pros and cons.

Fundamental Analysis: Digging into the Basics

Fundamental analysis is like a health checkup for a company: You review its "vitals" (financial statements) and environment (economy, industry) to see if it's strong or shaky. It's great for long-term investing, as it helps spot undervalued gems.

Macroeconomic Factors: Start broad. Key influences include:

1. **Fiscal Policy**: The government's taxing and spending. High taxes cut spending power; cuts boost it. For 2026, with federal deficits projected at around $65-$75 billion, watch for stimulus in housing or green tech.
2. **Monetary Policy**: Bank of Canada's interest rates. Low rates (like 2.25% in late 2025) make borrowing cheap, spurring growth; high rates cool inflation.
3. **Inflation**: Rising prices erode value. Target is 2%; if it hits 2.5% in 2026, it could squeeze profits. Add **ESG Factors** (Environmental, Social, Governance): Now essential for sustainability. Does the company cut emissions? Treat workers well? Have diverse boards? In 2025, sustainable funds returned 12.5% on average, vs. 9.2% for traditional funds—proof that ESG can boost returns.

Industry Analysis: Zoom in. Companies thrive (or struggle) based on their sector. Use the Global Industry Classification Standard (GICS): 11 sectors (e.g., Energy, Tech), 25 groups, 74 industries, 163 sub-industries. For example, Ontario's auto sector (like in Windsor) is facing EV shifts—check whether a company like Magna is adapting.

Company Life Cycle: Industries evolve in stages—use this to gauge growth potential:

Stage	Characteristics	Example (Ontario Focus)	Risk/Growth
Emerging Growth	New products, low profits, but high potential. High risk.	Tech startups in Toronto's Kitchener-Waterloo hub, like AI firms.	High growth, very high risk.
Growth	Rapid sales/ earnings, reinvests cash. "Growth stocks."	Shopify (Ottawa-based), expanding e-commerce.	High growth, moderate risk.
Mature	Steady growth, stable dividends. "Income stocks."	Enbridge pipelines serving Ontario.	Low growth, low risk.
Decline	Falling demand (e.g., due to tech changes). Steady cash but shrinking profits.	Traditional manufacturing in Windsor is hit by automation.	Low growth, high risk of obsolescence.

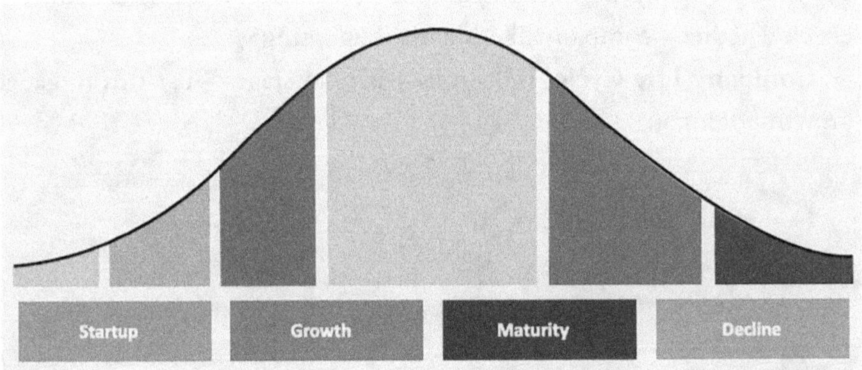

Key Ratios: Crunch numbers from balance sheets (assets/liabilities snapshot), income statements (profits over time), and cash flow statements (actual money movement). These are like vital signs for a company's health—quick checks to see if it's thriving or wheezing. You can find them free on sites like Yahoo Finance (finance.yahoo.com), TMX Money (money.tmx.com), or Morningstar.ca—just search the stock ticker (e.g., "TD.TO" for TD Bank) and look under "Key Statistics" or "Financials." Let's break down the big three with analogies and examples.

Price-to-Earnings (P/E) Ratio: This is simply the stock price divided by earnings per share (EPS)—in other words, how much you're shelling out for each dollar of the company's profit. Think of it like deciding if a coffee shop is overpriced: If one charges $20 for a cup that nets them $1 in profit (P/E=20), it feels steep compared to another spot charging $10 for the same $1 profit (P/E=10). It's a quick way to spot potential bargains or red flags. As of December 19, 2025, the S&P/TSX Composite's P/E sits at about ~20. If a stock's P/E dips below this benchmark (or its industry average), it might be undervalued—like finding that hidden gem cafe with great value. A higher P/E could hint at strong growth ahead (common in tech) or just plain overvaluation. For example, imagine a stock trading at $50 with $5 EPS—that's a P/E of 10. If the industry norm is 20, you're essentially paying half price per profit dollar, which could be a win... but always dig deeper, as a low P/E might flag risks like sluggish growth or market headwinds.

Behavioural tip: Don't chase ultra-low P/E without digging—it's like buying a cheap house without inspecting the foundation.

Debt-to-Equity (D/E) Ratio: Total debt divided by shareholders' equity (owner's stake after liabilities). It's a leverage check: How much the company borrows vs. owns outright. Under 1 is healthy (mostly self-funded, like a home with a small mortgage); over 2 might mean risk if rates rise. Measure it via the same sites—under "Balance Sheet." Example: If debt is $500M and equity $1B, D/E=0.5 (solid). Banks often have higher (5-10) due to their business, but compare within industries. In Canada, with prime rates at ~4.45%, high D/E could hurt if borrowing costs climb.

Return on Equity (ROE): Net income divided by shareholders' equity—shows how efficiently profits are generated from owners' money. Aim for 15%+ (strong performers like a business turning $1 invested into $1.15

profit yearly). Find it in the "Key Ratios" section online. Example: 20% ROE means solid management; below 10% might flag inefficiencies. Tie it to ESG: Companies with high ROE often score well on governance, like transparent boards.

Action item: Pull up a TSX stock on Yahoo Finance today—calculate P/E manually (price ÷ EPS) to practice.

Example: Let's follow Alex, our young Toronto renter, as he analyzes TD Bank (ticker: TD.TO) for his RRSP. He starts broadly: Banking is a mature industry in Canada, with steady demand but facing fintech competition (like apps eating into fees). Using Yahoo Finance, Alex sees TD's P/E at ~10.7—well below the TSX average of around 20, suggesting it's undervalued compared to peers like RBC (~12). D/E is high (typical for banks at around 17x, as they leverage deposits), and ROE is a healthy 16.91%—showing good profit from equity despite U.S. expansion costs. ESG shines: TD aims for net-zero emissions by 2050, with green lending programs aligning with Ontario's push for sustainable finance. In the mature life-cycle stage, TD offers reliable dividends (yield ~3.3%), perfect for Alex's long-term goals. It's like a solid condo in Toronto—undervalued now due to market dips, but with strong foundations and eco-upgrades, it'll appreciate. Alex decides it's a solid pick but diversifies to mitigate bank-specific risks, such as rate changes.

Technical Analysis: Reading the Market's Mood

Technical analysis is like weather forecasting: It uses charts to spot patterns, ignoring "why" for "what's happening now." Ideal for short-term trades.

Chart Analysis: Visuals show price history over time, helping spot trends.

Bar charts use vertical lines to mark the high and low prices for a period (like a day), with short horizontal ticks on the left for the opening price and on the right for the closing price.

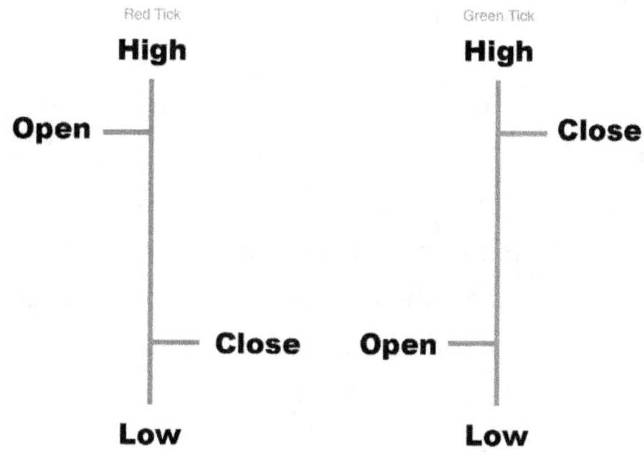

Candlestick charts build on this for more insight: Each "candle" has a rectangular body (thick part, typically green if the price closed higher than it opened—showing gains—or red if lower, indicating losses) representing the open-to-close range, and thin wicks (also called shadows) extending above and below for the full high/low extremes. Patterns matter: A long lower wick might suggest buyers stepped in after a dip (potential reversal), while a small body with long wicks signals indecision.

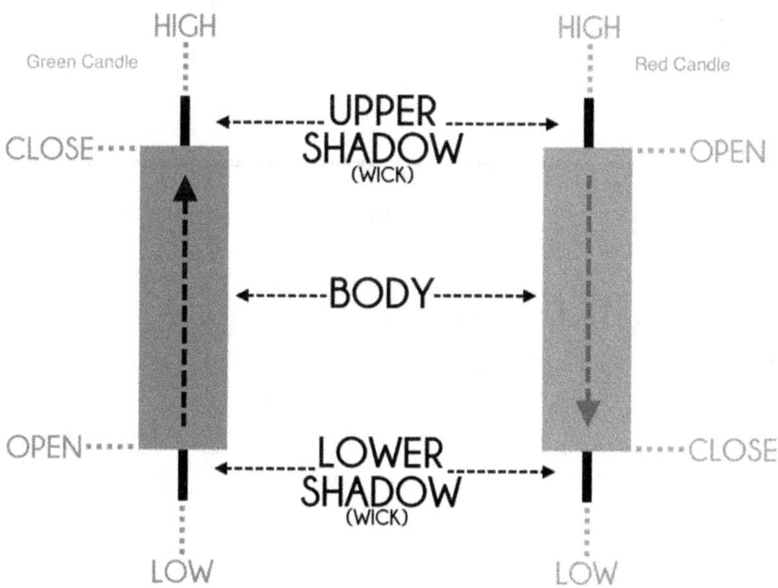

Support/Resistance: Support acts like a floor, where the price tends to bounce back up after a dip—buyers jump in, thinking it's a good deal. Resistance is a ceiling where the price struggles to break higher—sellers take profits, halting the rise. If the price breaks through resistance (with strong volume), it signals a potential uptrend change; dropping below support might mean a downtrend. Example: If a stock hovers at $50 support and bounces multiple times, but then falls to $48, watch for sellers dominating. Think of support as a trampoline catching falls, and resistance as a lid on a pot—pop it off, and things heat up!

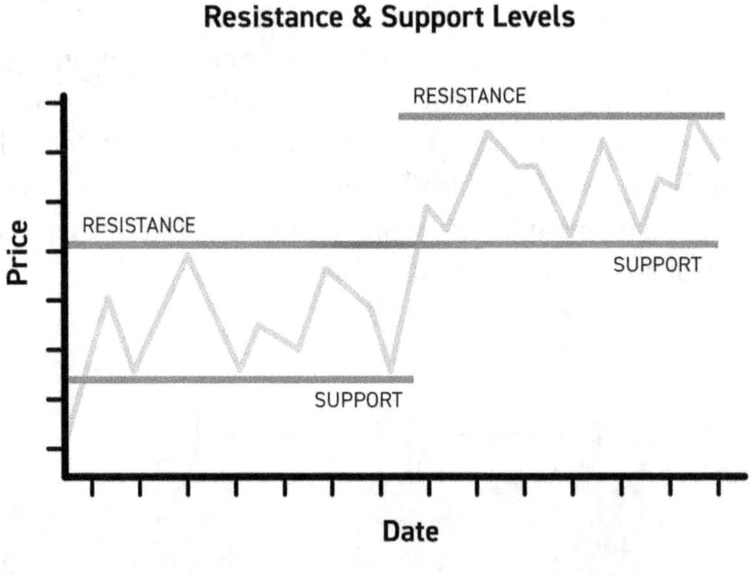

Quantitative Tools: Smooth data with moving averages (MA). 50-day MA: Average of the last 50 closes. Price above MA? Buy signal.

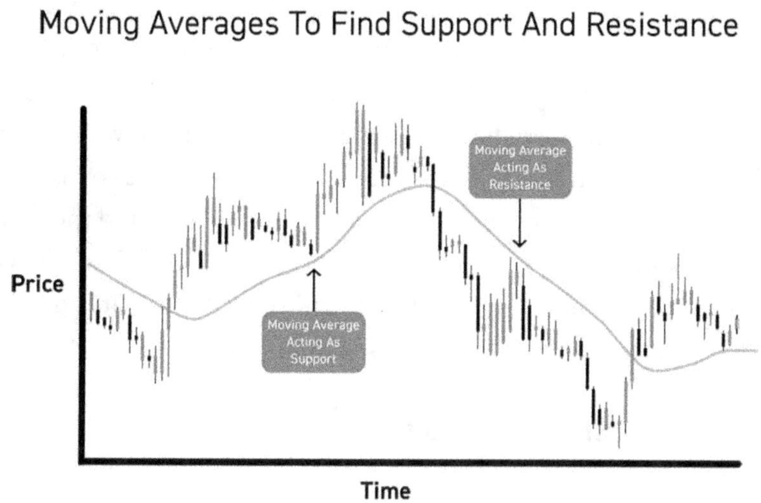

Sentiment Indicators: These tools gauge the "crowd mood" or overall investor emotion toward a stock or market, often revealing extremes that signal reversals. Common ones include bull/bear ratios (percentage of optimistic vs. pessimistic sentiment) or put/call ratios (high put volume suggests fear). Pull them from sites like Yahoo Finance, CNN Fear & Greed Index, or StockTwits. If 80%+ are bullish, it might signal overbought conditions—too much hype —so consider selling before a dip; conversely, extreme bearishness could signal a buy opportunity. Example: If Shopify (SHOP.TO) shows 85% bullish sentiment amid e-commerce buzz, Priya might trim her RESP holdings to lock in gains. It's like checking party vibes—if everyone's euphoric and dancing wildly, the fun might end soon; if gloomy, a turnaround could spark energy!

Cycle Analysis: Markets have natural rhythms or patterns that repeat over time, influenced by economic, seasonal, or behavioural factors—think of them as waves in the ocean, rising and falling in predictable patterns. Key types include long-term cycles (2+ years, like business expansions/ contractions), intermediate (months, e.g., quarterly earnings impacts), short-term (weeks/days, from news events), and seasonal (e.g., holiday shopping boosts retail stocks in Q4, or "sell in May and go away" for summer dips). Always use this with other tools like charts, for confirmation, as cycles aren't foolproof. Example: The TSX often sees the energy sector gains in winter due to heating demand—Alex might time his buys accordingly. It's like predicting traffic patterns; rush hour (seasonal peaks) is reliable, but accidents (unexpected events) can disrupt—plan around the rhythms but stay flexible!

AI twist: Tools now use machine learning to detect patterns, like in apps that spot sentiment in news. Use Grok to learn more.

Strategies for Smart Analysis

Combine Approaches: Use fundamentals for "what to buy," technicals for "when." Alex picks growth stocks via ratios, and times buys on charts.

Incorporate Sustainability: Add ESG screens—check Morningstar for ratings.

Diversify Analysis: Don't rely on one tool; cross-check.

Analysis isn't magic—it's like dating: Check compatibility (fundamentals) and vibes (technicals) before committing!

Potential Risks and How to Mitigate Them

Overreliance on Past Data: Markets change; mitigate by staying up to date on current news.

Emotional Biases: FOMO buys high; set rules like "only buy if P/E <15."

Info Overload: Start simple; use tools to filter.

2026 Risks: Geopolitical tensions or AI bubbles—diversify and review quarterly.

Behavioural tip: Journal your decisions to spot patterns, like impulsively chasing trends.

Self-Check Quiz

Quick test—answers at the end:

1. What does a low P/E suggest? (A) Overvalued (B) Undervalued (C) Irrelevant
2. True/False: Technical analysis ignores company finances.
3. Name one ESG factor.
4. In which life cycle stage are dividends steady? (A) Emerging (B) Mature (C) Decline

If aligned, great; otherwise, review above.
Answers: 1. B, 2, True, 3, e.g., Environmental impact, 4. B

Tools and Next Steps

Beginner Apps: Morningstar.ca for ESG ratings and ratios; Yahoo Finance for free charts; TMX Money (tsx.com) for TSX data.

Advanced: Finbox or Koyfin for deeper analysis; AI like Grok for quick insights (but verify!).

Government Resources: CRA's investor education - securities-administrators.ca/investor-tools/understanding-your-investments/types-of-investments/.

Action Item: Practice on a paper trading (Trading Simulator) - track 3 stocks for a month.

Conclusion

Investment analysis demystifies the market, turning guesses into strategies. Whether you're like Jordan (a Windsor retiree), seeking a stable income or Alex chasing growth, these tools empower you. Remember, it's a marathon—start small, learn from dips, and adjust. Up next: Taxes, where we tie it all together. You've got this—keep analyzing!

Chapter 16

The Fundamentals of Canadian Taxation

Taxes in Canada fund public services, and for individuals, they're primarily on income—think of it as the government taking a slice of your earnings pie. The system is progressive, meaning higher earners pay a higher rate on portions of their income, like climbing a ladder where each rung costs more. It's split between federal (national) and provincial/territorial (e.g., Ontario adds its own layer). You file one return to the CRA, which handles both.

Key income types taxed differently:

- **Employment Income**: Wages, salaries—taxed at full rates.
- **Investment Income**: Varies—interest like regular income, dividends with perks, capital gains only half-taxed.
- **Other**: Self-employment, rentals—similar to employment but with deductions.

Everyone gets a basic personal amount (BPA)—a chunk of income that's tax-free to cover essentials, like a "free pass" on your first bit of earnings. For 2026 federally, it's up to $16,452 if your net income is $181,440 or less (full credit), phasing out gradually to $14,829 for incomes between $181,441 and $258,482 (partial credit), and zero beyond that. Ontario has its own BPA of $12,989 for 2026 (indexed ~2% from 2025), which works similarly but doesn't phase out—it's a flat amount for all, reducing your provincial tax.

Imagine your income as a pizza—the government takes slices based on size, but you get free toppings (deductions) to reduce the bill.

Behavioural tip: Don't fear taxes; view them as a tool—deductions reward wise choices like saving in an RRSP.

Tax Brackets and Rates

Your tax rate applies only to income in each bracket—not your whole pot. For 2026, figures are indexed by 2.0% for inflation. Here's a federal table (note: lowest rate drops to 14% from 15% in 2025, effective full-year 2026):

Bracket	Taxable Income Range	Rate
1	Up to $58,523	14%
2	$58,524 to $117,045	20.5%
3	$117,046 to $181,440	26%
4	$181,441 to $258,482	29%
5	Over $258,482	33%

For Ontario (projected 2026, indexed ~2% from 2025):

Bracket	Taxable Income Range	Rate
1	Up to $53,891	5.05%
2	$53,892 to $107,785	9.15%
3	$107,786 to $150,000	11.16%
4	$150,001 to $220,000	12.16%
5	Over $220,000	13.16%

Plus Ontario surtax: This is an extra layer on your basic provincial tax (not income), like a "fee on top of the bill." It's 20% on basic tax over $5,936 (projected 2026 threshold, indexed), and an additional 36% on basic tax over $7,589—totalling up to 56% surtax on the excess, pushing effective top rates higher. Combined federal + Ontario: Effective marginal rates start around 19.05% (14% fed + 5.05% ON) for low earners and top out at ~53.53% for high incomes (33% fed + 13.16% ON + full surtax impact).

Example: Let's take a closer look at how taxes might play out for Alex, our young Toronto renter earning $60,000 annually (assuming this is his taxable income after any basic deductions). This table breaks it down step by step, showing federal and provincial (Ontario) calculations before credits, then the impact of Basic Personal Amounts (BPAs). Remember, this is an approximation for illustration—taxes can vary based on other credits, deductions, or factors like CPP/EI contributions. Always plug your numbers into the CRA's online tax calculator for precision.

Tax Authority	Bracket	Income in Bracket	Rate	Tax Amount	Subtotal Before Credits
Federal	1st (Up to $58,523)	$58,523	14%	~$8,193	-
Federal	2nd ($58,524–$117,045)	$1,477	20.5%	~$303	~$8,496
Ontario	1st (Up to $53,891)	$53,891	5.05%	~$2,721	-
Ontario	2nd ($53,892–$107,785)	$6,109	9.15%	~$559	~$3,280
Combined Before Credits	-	-	-	-	~$11,776

BPA Adjustments and Final Estimates

- **Federal BPA**: Reduces your effective taxable income by up to ~$16,452 (for incomes under $181,440), equivalent to a tax credit of about $2,303 (at 14% rate).
- **Ontario BPA**: Reduces your effective taxable income by up to ~$12,989, equivalent to a tax credit of about $656 (at 5.05% rate).
- **Total Tax After BPAs (approx.)**: Drops to ~$9,500–$10,000 (varies with other credits like climate action incentives or employment amounts; no surtax applies here as Ontario tax is below thresholds).
- **Estimated Take-Home Pay**: ~$50,000 (after taxes, before other payroll deductions like CPP/EI).

Pro Tip: If your income is similar, focus on maxing out deductions (e.g., RRSP contributions) to lower your taxable base even more.

Taxation of Investments

Investments aren't taxed equally—this is key to smart planning. All investments outside registered accounts, such as TFSA (tax-free) or RRSP (deferred tax).

Interest Income (e.g., GICs, bonds): Taxed as regular income at your marginal rate. Example: $1,000 interest at a 25% bracket = $250 tax.

Dividends: Canadian eligible dividends (from large public companies) get a **gross-up** (38% boost to $138 for a $100 dividend), but a tax credit (15.02% federal, plus provincial) lowers the effective rate. This "gross-up" pretends the dividend is higher to match the corporate tax paid, then credits it back, making the effective tax low (even negative for basics). Non-eligible dividends (from small businesses) have a 15% gross-up ($115 for $100) and a lower credit (~9% federal), so a slightly higher effective tax, but still preferential. The effective rate can range from 0% to 10% for low earners.

Capital Gains: Only 50% taxable. $10,000 gain = $5,000 taxed at your marginal rate. Capital losses (from selling at a loss) offset gains: First, reduce current-year gains to zero; excess can be carried back 3 years (claim a refund) or forward indefinitely to future gains—handy for balancing bumpy markets.

Foreign investments: U.S. dividends withhold 15% (unless held in RRSP—treaty reduces to 0% in RRSP), recoverable by claiming a foreign tax credit (FTC) on your Canadian income tax return, which mitigates double taxation.

In registered accounts:

TFSA: contributions are not deductible, but all growth (interest, dividends, gains) and withdrawals are tax-free forever; ideal for flexible savings.

RRSP: contributions are deductible (reduce current taxable income), growth is tax-deferred (no tax until withdrawn), but withdrawals are taxed as income (usually in retirement at a lower rate); early withdrawals face withholding tax.

FHSA: like RRSP (deductible contributions, deferred growth) but tax-free qualified withdrawals for first home; penalties for non-qualified use.

RESP: contributions not deductible, but attract grants (CESG up to 20%), growth tax-deferred, withdrawals taxed to beneficiary (student, often low/no tax).

These are "tax shelters"—TFSA like a free-growth greenhouse, RRSP a deferral vault.

Example: Priya sells stocks for a $5,000 gain in her non-registered account—$2,500 taxed at her 26% rate (~$650). In TFSA? Zero tax.

Deductions and Credits

Deductions reduce taxable income; credits cut tax owed directly. Claim via T1 form.

Common deductions:

Credits (non-refundable unless noted): Non-refundable credits reduce your tax bill but can't create a refund if they exceed what you owe—like a discount coupon up to the total cost. Refundable ones can give cash back even if the tax is zero, like a rebate.

Canada Child Benefit: Up to about $7,997/child under 6 (income-tested, refundable).

GST/HST Credit: Quarterly payments for low-income (~$500 single, refundable).

Climate Action Incentive: Ontario ~$1,000/family rebate for carbon tax (refundable).

Example: Jordan claims medical credits for $3,000 in expenses—reduces federal tax by 15% ($450 saved, non-refundable).

Action item: Log expenses year-round; use CRA's My Account to estimate.

Strategies for Minimizing Taxes

Smart planning = lower bill. Always legal—think optimizing, not evading.

Use Registered Accounts: RRSP for high earners. Deduct contributions now to lower current tax bracket, pay tax later in retirement when likely lower rate—great if you expect income drop; TFSA for flexibility (no deduction but tax-free everything, ideal for mid/low earners or emergency funds).

Income Splitting: Share income with family to use lower brackets—e.g., pension income split up to 50% with spouse (reduces total family tax).

Timing Gains: Sell losers to offset winners (harvest losses same year, or carry back/forward as needed—e.g., $5,000 capital loss wipes $5,000 capital gain before 50% inclusion).

Charitable Donations: Credit at 15% federal + provincial on first $200, up to 29-33% on excess (up to 75% of income limit; higher rates for large gifts over $200).

AI Tools: Apps like Wealthsimple Tax use AI to spot deductions.

Taxes are inevitable, but strategies are like coupons—why pay full price?

Filing, Deadlines, and Potential Risks

File by April 30 (June 15 for self-employed, but payment due April 30 to avoid interest). Keep records for 6 years from the end of the tax year.

Risks:

Underreporting: Penalties 10-50% + interest.

Late Filing: 5% penalty +1%/month.

Overclaiming: Audit triggers such as large deductions.

Mitigate: by double-checking using software; consult an accountant if complex. Use CRA pre-filled info when filing your taxes.

Behavioural tip: File early to avoid rush—treat it like budgeting. Plan ahead.

Self-Check Quiz

Quick test—answers at the end:

1. What's the federal tax rate on the first $58,523? (A) 14% (B) 20.5% (C) 26%
2. True/False: Only 50% of capital gains are taxable.
3. Name one common deduction.
4. What's a strategy for high earners? (A) TFSA only (B) RRSP contributions (C) Ignore taxes

If aligned, great; otherwise, review above.
Answers: 1. A, 2. True, 3. e.g., Medical expenses, 4. B

Tools and Next Steps

CRA My Account: Track refunds, pre-fill returns.

Apps: TurboTax, H&R Block - both are using AI assistance to help you with your tax filing.

Use Canada-certified tax software to find more apps to help you with your taxes- canada.ca/en/services/taxes/income-tax/personal-income-tax/how-file/tax-software/find-software.html

Next: Review last year's return; estimate 2026 taxes with TurboTax or CRA calculator.

Conclusion

Taxes are part of the financial game, but with knowledge, you control the score. Whether Alex dodging brackets with RRSPs or Priya claiming child credits, smart tax moves build wealth. Remember, it's about fairness—use these tips to pay less legally and invest more. Up next: Crafting your portfolio to tie it all together. You've got this—file confidently!

Chapter 17

Crafting Your Investment Portfolio

You've made it to the final chapter—congrats! By now, you've got the tools: mindset, savings plans, investment basics, analysis skills, and even tax know-how. It's time to put it all together by crafting your investment portfolio. Think of a portfolio as your personal financial garden—you plant a mix of seeds (investments) suited to your soil (goals and risk level), water it regularly (add contributions), and prune as needed (rebalance). This isn't about picking hot stocks; it's about building a simple, diversified setup that grows steadily. We'll use our Ontario friends: Alex (Toronto renter chasing growth), Priya (Ottawa parent balancing family needs), and Jordan (Windsor retiree focusing on income). Updated for 2026 with projections like analysts expecting the S&P/TSX Composite to rise about 5% by year-end (from late-2025 levels), we'll keep it practical and encouraging. Remember, these are illustrative examples only, not investment advice. Past performance isn't indicative of future results, and markets can go down as well as up—always do your own research or consult a qualified advisor. Let's design your garden.

The Fundamentals of Crafting a Portfolio

A portfolio is simply your collection of investments—such as stocks, bonds, ETFs, or mutual funds—held in accounts like TFSA or RRSP. The goal? Grow your money over time while managing risk. It's not one-size-fits-all; it depends on your age, goals, and comfort with ups/downs (risk tolerance). For 2026, with steady GDP around 1.5% and inflation at ~2%, a balanced portfolio can aim for 4-7% annual returns, depending on your mix. As illustrated in the risk-return curve below, higher potential returns often come with more risk—starting from "Safety" (low risk, low return) up to "Growth" (higher risk, higher potential)—helping you pick a spot that matches your comfort level, like choosing a rollercoaster ride based on how much thrill you can handle.

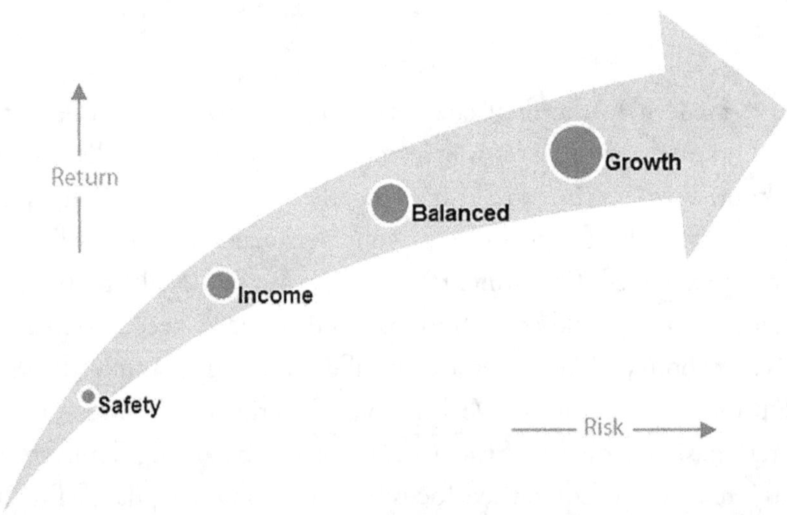

Key concepts:

Asset Allocation: How you divide your money across types (e.g., 60% stocks for growth, 40% bonds for stability). It's the biggest driver of returns—more than picking individual ones.

Diversification: Spreading bets so one bad apple doesn't spoil the bunch. Mix sectors, geographies, and types.

Risk Tolerance: Conservative? More bonds. Aggressive? More stocks. Assess via quizzes on sites like ciro.ca/office-investor/understanding-risk/investor-questionnaire.

It's like packing a lunch—proteins (stocks) for energy, veggies (bonds) for health, and a treat (crypto ETFs) for fun, portioned by your appetite (age/goals).

Behavioural tip: Avoid "recency bias"—don't chase last year's winners; stick to your plan.

Strategies for Building Your Portfolio

Start with your "why": Retirement? Home? Kids' education? Then allocate based on time horizon—longer time horizons mean more growth focus.

Age-Based Allocation Examples: A rule of thumb: Subtract your age from 110 for stock percentage (rest bonds/fixed). Adjust for risk. Here's a 2026 table with sustainable tweaks (e.g., 10-20% ESG funds for climate alignment, as sustainable assets globally edging up to about $3.7 trillion by late 2025, with strong growth in Canada). These are hypothetical illustrations; research specific options yourself.

Age Group	Sample Allocation	Example Investments (in TFSA/RRSP)	Why It Fits
20s-30s (e.g., Alex, growth-focused)	80-90% stocks/ETFs, 10-20% bonds, 5% crypto ETFs	50% broad Canadian equity ETF (tracking S&P/TSX Composite), 30% global stocks (e.g., diversified international index), 10% bonds (government/corporate mix), 5% cryptocurrency ETF, 5% ESG-focused ETF	High risk tolerance; time to recover dips.
40s-50s (e.g., Priya, balanced)	60-70% stocks, 30-40% bonds, 5-10% alternatives	40% mixed Canadian/ global equity ETF (broad market index), 30% bonds (aggregate bond index), 10% real estate REITs ETF, 10% ESG funds, 5% cryptocurrency ETF	Family priorities. Moderate growth with buffers.
60s+ (e.g., Jordan, income-oriented)	40-50% stocks, 50-60% bonds/ fixed, 5% cash	30% dividend-focused equity ETF (high-yield index), 50% bonds/GICs (broad bond index), 10% ESG bonds, 5% cash in HISA	Preserve capital; steady income. Low volatility.

Steps to Build:

1. **Assess Yourself**: Goals, timeline, risk (e.g., via Vanguard's quiz at vanguard.ca).
2. **Choose Accounts**: TFSA for flexibility, RRSP for tax breaks.
3. **Select Investments**: ETFs for low-cost diversity (MER ~0.2-0.5%). Add sustainable: ESG ETFs returned a median of ~12% in the first half of 2025, for illustration.

4. **Invest Gradually**: Dollar-cost average—buy monthly to smooth prices.
5. **Rebalance Annually**: Sell winners, buy laggards to maintain allocation. For example, if you aim for 60% stocks and 40% bonds but stocks grow to 65% (a 5% buffer shift), sell some stocks and buy bonds to reset—keeps risk in check without over-trading.

Example: Alex, 28, starts with $10,000 in TFSA: $7,000 in broad equity ETFs (e.g., tracking S&P/TSX or S&P 500 for diversity), $2,000 bonds, $1,000 ESG/crypto. He adds $500/month via auto-deposits. (This is just an example—tailor to your situation.)

Building a portfolio is like LEGO—start simple, add bricks as you gain confidence, but don't build a tower too tall without a base!

AI twist: Robo-advisors like Wealthsimple use AI to optimize allocations based on your profile.

Withdrawals and Tax Implications

Portfolios aren't set-it-forget-it—life happens, like needing cash for a home down payment or an emergency. Withdraw strategically to minimize taxes and penalties: Start with TFSA (all growth and withdrawals are entirely tax-free, no impact on income-tested benefits like OAS). Then, non-registered accounts (watch for capital gains tax on profits—only 50% taxable, but plan sales to stay in lower brackets). Save RRSP for last (withdrawals count as income, potentially pushing you into higher brackets and triggering withholding tax of 10-30%; ideal for retirement when income is lower). It's like unpacking a suitcase—grab the easy-access items (TFSA) first, save the bulky ones (RRSP) for when you settle in.

For 2026, with the capital gains inclusion rate at 50%, harvest losses yearly: Sell underperforming assets to offset gains, reducing your tax bill—like using a coupon to lower the cost of winners.

Rebalancing: Sell/buy to reset mix—do in tax-sheltered accounts like TFSA or RRSP to avoid triggering capital gains tax right away. Example: Priya rebalances her RESP annually (e.g., shifting from stocks to bonds as her kids near school age), keeping government grants intact and avoiding early withdrawal penalties.

Potential Risks and How to Mitigate Them

Market Volatility: The S&P/TSX could dip 10-20% during recessions, like in economic slowdowns—prices swing due to news or cycles. Mitigate: Diversify globally (e.g., add U.S./international ETFs), hold 3-6 months' expenses in cash for emergencies so you don't sell low.

Inflation Erosion: Around 2% annual inflation eats away at returns over time, reducing purchasing power. Add inflation-beaters like stocks/ETFs (which historically outpace inflation) or Treasury Inflation-Protected Securities (TIPS) bonds that adjust with price rises.

Over-Complication: Too many holdings? It can lead to confusion and higher fees—stick to 5-10 ETFs for simplicity and broad coverage.

2026 Risks: Geopolitical trade tensions or overhyped AI bubbles could spark sell-offs—keep 5-10% in defensive stocks/ETFs like utilities (stable sectors less affected by drama).

Behavioural tip: Ignore daily noise—zoom out like checking a plant's growth weekly, not hourly.

Self-Check Quiz

Quick test—answers at the end:

1. What's asset allocation? (A) Picking stocks (B) Dividing money across types (C) Timing markets
2. True/False: Diversification reduces risk.
3. For a 40-year-old, roughly what stock % is recommended? (A) 20% (B) 70% (C) 100%
4. Name a mitigation for volatility.

If aligned, great; otherwise, review above.
Answers: 1. B, 2. True, 3. B, 4. e.g., Diversify or hold cash

Tools and Next Steps

Beginner Apps: Wealthsimple (AI-driven), Questwealth (low fees ~0.25%). RBC InvestEase for bank integration.

Advanced: Questrade for self-directed; Morningstar.ca for investment insights.

Government Resources: CIRO investing basics guide ciro.ca/office-investor/investing-basics.

For beginners, consider mutual fund companies or meeting with a financial advisor to hear their insights—don't commit until you've spoken with a few (even over the phone). They can manage everything for you, though you'll pay a management fee; shop around to find a good fit.

Next: Book an appointment with a financial advisor at your bank or with an online brokerage such as Questrade or Wealthsimple to open a TFSA account and invest $100 or more in a broad ETF (e.g., tracking the S&P/TSX for Canadian exposure)—track for 3 months.

Conclusion

Crafting a portfolio is your roadmap to financial freedom—simple, diversified, and tailored. Whether Alex's growth tilt, Priya's balance, or Jordan's stability, start small and adjust as life evolves. You've got the knowledge; now act. Remember, investing is a marathon—consistent steps win. Thanks for joining this journey—here's to your brighter future! For more, check canada.ca/en/services/finance.html or revisit chapters. You've got this—grow on!

Conclusion

Wrapping It Up: Your Path to Financial Confidence

You've reached the end! Give yourself a pat on the back for making it through *Canadian Financial Mastery*. From shifting your money mindset in Chapter 1 to crafting a balanced portfolio in Chapter 17, we've covered the essentials: budgeting basics, tax-advantaged accounts like TFSAs and RRSPs, investment options from bonds to crypto ETFs, economic big pictures, analysis tools, taxes, and more. Think back to our Ontario friends—Alex turning his Toronto rent challenges into smart TFSA savings, Priya juggling Ottawa family life with RESPs for her kids, and Jordan securing Windsor retirement income through steady bonds. Their stories show it's doable, no matter your starting point.

The key takeaway? Personal finance isn't about getting rich quickly—it's about small, consistent steps that compound over time, like interest on a GIC. You've got the knowledge to break free from debt stress, build wealth sustainably, and navigate 2026's landscape (with steady 1.5% GDP growth and ~2% inflation as a backdrop). Remember, challenges like rising costs are normal, but with a positive mindset and these strategies, you're equipped to handle them. As we touched on, ESG investing and

AI tools, the future's bright—focus on what you can control, like your habits and choices.

If finance were a road trip from Toronto to Vancouver, you've just fueled up and mapped the route—no more wrong turns into debt ditches!

Next Steps: Turning Knowledge into Action

Don't let this book gather dust—start small today. Here's a practical roadmap:

- **Review and Reflect**: Revisit your money mindset (Ch1). Jot down one limiting belief and replace it with a positive affirmation, like "I'm building wealth one step at a time."
- **Build Your Foundation**: Set up a budget using the 50/30/20 rule (Ch1). Aim to save 10-20% of income.
- **Open Key Accounts**: If eligible, start a TFSA or RRSP (Ch3-4). Contribute what you can— even $50/month adds up.
- **Invest Wisely**: Analyze one simple ETF (Ch15) and add to your portfolio (Ch17). Rebalance quarterly to stay on track.
- **Tax Check**: Estimate your 2026 taxes with CRA's calculator. Claim deductions like medical expenses (Ch16).
- **Stay Educated**: Monitor economic cycles (Ch14) via Bank of Canada updates (bankofcanada.ca). Adjust for interest rate changes (Ch13).
- **Action Item:** Pick one goal (e.g., $5,000 emergency fund) and break it into monthly steps. Track progress—celebrate wins!

Behavioural tip: Progress beats perfection— if you slip (like an impulse buy), learn and move on, no self-judgment.

Feel free to contact me on social media - @AdiMalihi

Mindset and Goals Tracker

Date: ______________________________

My top 3 financial goals (SMART: Specific, Measurable, Achievable, Relevant, Time-bound):

1.

2.

3.

Limiting belief I'm shifting: ______________________________

____

____

____

New affirmation: ______________________________

____

____

____

Wins this week/month: ______________________________

____

____

____

Notes/reflections: ______________________________

____

____

Budget and Savings Log

Date: ______________________________

Monthly income (after-tax): $______________________________

Expenses (use 50/30/20 above to allocate):

Needs: $__________ (list key items:
______________________________)

Wants: $__________ (list key items:
______________________________)

Savings/Debt: $__________ (list key items:
______________________________)

Savings contributions this month:

TFSA: $__________

RRSP: $__________

FHSA/RESP: $__________

Other (e.g., non-registered): $__________

Emergency fund progress:

Current balance: $__________

Goal: $__________ (e.g., 3-6 months' expenses)

Notes on progress: ______________________________
____

General notes: (e.g., "Cut coffee runs—saved $50! What worked? Adjustments for next month?")

____

____

Financial Successes Journal

Remember back in Chapter 1, where we talked about cultivating a positive money mindset? One of the best ways to reinforce those good vibes is by celebrating your wins—no matter how small. This journal page is your space to track financial successes, big or small, like paying off a credit card, hitting a savings milestone, or even just sticking to your budget for a week. Write them down here to see how far you've come and keep that momentum going. Feel free to photocopy this page or use a notebook if you need more room.

Date	Success Description	How It Makes Me Feel	Next Step Inspired By This

Pro tip: Review this journal monthly. It's like giving yourself a high-five and reminding your brain that progress is happening. You've got this—keep building that wealth!

General Notes

Date: ______________________________

Use this space for anything—key takeaways from the book, questions to ask an advisor, new ideas sparked by chapters, or even sketches of your financial roadmap. Prompts to get started:

What surprised me most?

____

____

____

One change I'll make this year:

____

____

____

____

Resources to explore next:

____

____

____

____

Other thoughts/doodles:

____

____

____

www.ingramcontent.com/pod-product-compliance
Lightning Source LLC
LaVergne TN
LVHW022059200926
848481LV00003B/986
* 9 7 8 1 7 3 8 3 9 6 9 1 7 *